Physical Characteristics of the Irish Wolfhound
(from the American Kennel Club breed standard)

Back: Rather long than short.

Tail: Long and slightly curved.

Hair: Rough and hard on body, legs and head.

Hindquarters: Muscular thighs and second thigh long and strong as in the Greyhound.

Belly: Well drawn up.

Color and Markings: Gray, brindle, red, black, pure white, fawn or any other color that appears in the Deerhound.

Feet. arched and clos

Irish Wolfhound

By Alice Kane

Contents

KENNEL CLUB BOOKS® **IRISH WOLFHOUND**
ISBN: 1-59378-311-6

Copyright © 2005 • Kennel Club Books, LLC
308 Main Street, Allenhurst, NJ 07711 USA
Cover Design Patented: US 6,435,559 B2 • Printed in South Korea

Photography by Cheryl A. Ertelt
with additional photographs by:

Tom Booth, Paulette Braun, T.J. Calhoun, Alan and Sandy Carey, Carolina Biological Supply, Isabelle Français, Gilbert Studios, Carol Ann Johnson, Bill Jonas, Dr. Dennis Kunkel, Tam C. Nguyen, Phototake, Jean Claude Revy, Kent Standerford, Chuck Tatham and Alice van Kempen.

Illustrations by Patricia Peters.

The publisher wishes to thank all of the owners whose dogs are featured in this book, including Kathy Bagi, Jill Richards Bregy, Sheri Day, Sam Ewing, Aimee Felger, Patricia Grove, Megan Krejcik, Barbara Meadows, Gail Selsmeyer, Judith Simon, Dr. Lynn Simon, Lois Thomasson and Cyndi & Bernie Westhoff.

The Irish Wolfhound has a rich history in the UK. Mrs. I. H. Barr from Dorking, Surrey, England had a fine kennel of Irish Wolfhounds during the 1930s. Here is a veritable pack photographed with Mrs. Barr's young daughter.

HISTORY OF THE
IRISH WOLFHOUND

INTRODUCING THE IRISH WOLFHOUND

I will give thee a hound that was given to me in Ireland; he is big, and no worse than a stout man. Besides it is part of his nature that he has a man's wit, and he will bay at every man he knows to be thy foe, but never at thy friends. He can see, too, in any man's face whether he means thee well or ill, and he will lay down his life to be true to thee.

In the ninth or tenth century, when the dog served man, Scandinavian folklore records Olaf, Norwegian son of an Irish princess, describing his Irish Wolfhounds with fierce love and admiration. Today, when man serves the dog (a mutually agreeable arrangement!), Wolfhound enthusiasts echo Olaf's eloquence with modern-day tributes to Ireland's fearless and devoted sighthounds. A giant in size with a heart to match, the Irish Wolfhound is by nature gentle and a gentleman. Proud to give his heart to the hunt, he would sooner give it to you. Give him yours in return and you will

Reinagle's *Irish Wolfhound* was produced in 1803 when the breed was considered extinct. The painting was originally titled *The Irish Greyhound,* though it clearly depicts a Wolfhound.

were then called, in ancient Rome. Around 391 AD, Roman Consul Quintus Aurelius Symmachus is said to have thanked his brother Flavianus for his gift of Irish hounds, the first such dogs ever seen in the great city of Rome. They were brought there to fight in arena games, where their great size evoked excitement, but it was their gentle, friendly temperaments that truly astonished the Romans. The appearance of these large Celtic hounds in Rome suggests that the Wolfhound was considered a prized gift from Ireland to dignitaries of other countries.

The history of the breed in Ireland is well documented. From the first century AD, there are many tales of prized giant dogs, fearless and heroic, on deer hunts and in battle. Descriptions of these early Irish Wolfhounds purportedly were written by the third- or fourth-century Gaelic poet Oisin, son of the hunter and warrior Finn mac Coul, chief of King Cormac's household and master of his hounds. Naming 300

have a friend for life. The breed's history, characteristics, care and training are all here for you to enjoy—to whet your appetite for everything you need to know to be the best possible companion to the aristocratic, devoted Irish Wolfhound.

ESTABLISHMENT OF A NOBLE BREED

What a rich history has been recorded about the noble Irish Wolfhound! Early illustrations and reports of the breed may vary considerably, but there can be little doubt of its great antiquity. Wonderful myths and legends immortalize the breed's earliest beginnings in Ireland. There is even evidence of Irish Wolfhounds, or Wolfdogs, as they

ANCIENT RUNNING HOUNDS
Hunting dogs resembling Irish Wolfhounds were reported to exist in Greece and Cyprus around 1400 BC. Ancient Greeks and Romans spoke of the prowess and spectacle of these Gaelic and Celtic hounds in the chase and on the battlefield.

of these hounds in his verses, Oisin praised not only the strength and speed of these dogs but also the wisdom and affection of the breed.

By the ninth century AD, with the Danes' invasion of Ireland, these Irish dogs became known throughout Scandinavia. More and more references to Wolfdogs were found in Christian art and written works, and two Greyhounds are depicted in the *Book of Kells*. As the dogs' fame spread, they were no longer solely the war dogs of Irish chieftains. Kings and dignitaries from many different countries vied for Ireland's aristocratic hounds. King John of England presented one to Llewellyn, Prince of Wales, in 1210. Henry VIII, decades later, requested the breed, and a brace was also sent to Queen Elizabeth I. Gelert, the brave hound depicted in The Hon. W. R. Spencer's poem as "a lamb at home" and "a lion in the chase," further popularized the Wolfhound with his fearless kill of a wolf attacking his master's child. The demand for the Wolfhound soon followed. Successive generations of emperors, cardinals and kings continued to covet the dogs' prowess as hunters and devotion to their masters, and, by the late 1700s, admirers of the breed bemoaned its scarcity and feared that the few remaining hounds could be the last of their breed.

CANIS LUPUS

"Grandma, what big teeth you have!" The gray wolf, a familiar figure in fairy tales and legends, has had its reputation tarnished and its population pummeled over the centuries. Yet it is the descendants of this much-feared creature to which we open our homes and hearts. Our beloved dog, *Canis domesticus*, derives directly from the gray wolf, a highly social canine that lives in elaborately structured packs. In the wild, the gray wolf can range from 60 to 175 pounds, standing between 25 and 40 inches in height.

Thanks to those devoted fanciers, a revival of the breed took place in the 1800s. Preservation and restoration of the Irish Wolfhound required taking into account past inbreeding of native hunting dogs with Ireland's Wolfhound. There was also discussion of the strong similarity between the Irish Wolfhound and the Scottish Deerhound. Were the Wolfhound and the Scottish Deerhound really the same breed with only minor differences? Were they truly smooth-coated or rough-coated?

During this period, Archibald Hamilton Rowan claimed to have

Proud, tall and 100% Irish, the Wolfhound is the mascot of the Irish Guards.

the "last of the race" of true Irish Wolfdogs. His dog Bran, found in the pedigrees of many current-day Irish Wolfhounds, was bred by Mr. Carter and H. D. Richardson, two gentlemen working to prevent the extinction of the breed. It is said that Richardson's writings about the Irish Wolfdog greatly influenced Captain G. A. Graham, to whom the modern Wolfhound owes its survival. For years, he worked with larger-sized Deerhounds, seeking to, as he said, "recover" the Wolfdog in its original form. There was also some careful crossing of Borzoi and Great Dane stock. While Richardson noted that few specimens of the true Wolfdog breed still existed, he worked closely with the stock of Sir John Power of Kilfane and Whyte Baker of Ballytobin Castle. Using probably the purest blood strains still in existence, these two Irishmen were breeding toward the old type.

Eng. Ch. Gareth, owned by Mr. A. S. Hall, was one of the celebrated progeny of the famed Dermot Astore, considered to be the best Wolfhound in the UK in the mid-1930s.

OUT-OF-SIGHT CHAMPION AND SIRE

Eng. Ch. Conncara was one of Britain's greatest sires ever in the breed. He was 36 inches tall and much admired for his type and soundness; it was only when he retired from the show ring that it was revealed that he was blind. Throughout his stud career, he never sired a blind puppy and was responsible for many great champions.

Working for the breed for nearly half a century, Captain Graham collected pedigrees of nearly 300 Wolfdogs. He produced his own story on the Irish Wolfhound in 1879, the same year that the Irish Kennel Club held its first class for the breed. He founded the Irish Wolfhound Club in 1885 and served as its president until his death in 1908. He and his colleague, Major Garnier, another preservationist of the breed, compiled in 1886 the standard of points for the Irish Wolfdog. Adopted by the club, it is virtually the same breed standard that exists in the breed's homeland today. By 1879, The Kennel Club of England admitted the Irish Wolfhound into its registry, while in America the first two Irish Wolfhounds were registered.

The Scottish Deerhound, a fellow giant hound breed, might well have been the basis for the revival of the modern Irish Wolfhound, thanks to Captain G. A. Graham.

Captain Graham's ideal hound, and perhaps one of the finest breed examples of the early 20th century, was a champion named Cotswold of Mrs. Percy Shewell's Cotswold kennels. This was a beautiful, impressively sized dog that was undefeated in the show ring. Out of the same dam came another champion, Cotswold Patricia, also a model Wolfhound who dominated the show ring.

One of the most influential kennels early in the 20th century was Mr. Everett's Felixstowe. Leaving Ireland for Suffolk, England, his hounds were prized for their type, size and soundness, and like Captain Graham, his predecessor, he was devoted to the breed's survival. Felixstowe Kilcullen was a champion and one of Mr. Everett's top hounds; his stock, the foundation of many

kennels, can be traced to pedigrees today.

The Irish Wolfhound flourished after World War I, conscientiously nurtured by skilled and devoted breeders and kennels. At that time, more and more hounds were exported around the world, many to the United States, where interest mounted quickly. Popularity surged with the exportation of Sulhamstead Dan, a very influential hound in his new country, although Irish Wolfhounds were said to have been exported to the US a century earlier. By the 20th century, Wolfhounds traced to Captain Graham's venerable pedigree book were reportedly being bred. In 1927, the Irish Wolfhound Club of America was sanctioned by the American Kennel Club, the presiding dog club of the US.

OVER 34 INCHES OF ATHLETE!

One of the finest and biggest hounds of the very early 20th century was Mrs. Percy Shewell's Ch. Cotswold. Measuring over 34 inches, he is said to have chased a stray stag for 6 miles, stopping only when the deer leapt a wall 7 feet high. Coursing a hare, this same dog once effortlessly cleared a five-barred gate. He proved to many a doubter that the Irish Wolfhound's great size is no impediment to his athleticism!

Back in Britain, at that time, the breed was in demand and filling the nation's show rings. Sound in body and temperament, the Wolfhound was finally being celebrated for its impressive origins as a hunter. In 1924, the British Wolfhound Coursing Club was formed, holding competitions for the age-old sport of coursing (hare, not wolves!). Even long-time breeders, experts on the Wolfhound's attributes, were fascinated by the agility and remarkable speeds that their massive dogs could reach. The Irish Wolfhound in Britain was truly in its prime.

However, the ravages of World War II saw a sad decline in the breed. Nationwide chaos and food shortages decimated stock and valuable bloodlines. No new dogs' names were recorded in the English Kennel Club's Stud Book until 1948, when very limited breeding slowly resumed, led by a few determined breeders. Quality and soundness were desperately sought via a good outcross bloodline. British fanciers were therefore delighted by the 1951 importation of Rory of Kihone, a magnanimous gift sent by Miss F. Jeannette McGregor from America to revitalize the breed. Rory

Eng. Ch. Ivan Turgeneff, owned by the Duchess of Newcastle, was a typical Borzoi. This breed's close relationship to the Irish Wolfhound is not contested. Painting by Maud Earl.

Eng. Ch. Lady of Raikeshill, born in 1926, first started winning in 1927 and became a champion in 1928.

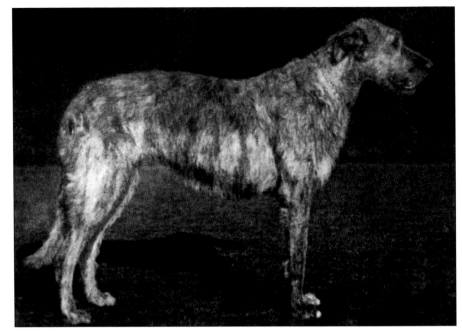

produced quality hounds with vastly improved temperament, while another US import, Ch. Cragwood Barney O'Shea of Riverlawn, passed on his formidable size and appearance. The conformation, quality, type and size of the Irish Wolfhound were revived, bringing new vitality into the breed and new dreams for its breeders.

THE IRISH WOLFHOUND IN ITS HOMELAND

While many nations have adopted the Irish Wolfhound, Ireland, of course, has its native breed embedded deep in its heart and history. Probably the most important and influential breeder,

historically, is Sheelagh Seale of Ballykelly kennels. She was introduced to the breed in the 1930s, and her hounds became the basis of renowned kennels throughout the world. Her first hound and foundation bitch was Avoca of Coolafin, a line-bred granddaughter of the famous Granua, known in the 1920s as the last pure-bred specimen of her race. Her most influential stud dog, Int. Ch. McGilligan of Ballykelly, born in 1957, is behind almost all of Ireland's hounds today. Her stock of mostly cream or wheaten hounds was prized for substance, soundness and impressive size. Her breeding continues through all of her champions' offspring

In a painting made especially for the famous dog book *Hutchinson's Popular and Illustrated Dog Encyclopaedia*, Nina Scott-Langley painted these Irish Wolfhounds. The breed was called "the most powerful dog in the world...nearly three feet in height."

A black and tan Irish Wolfhound of yesteryear, named Felixstowe Yirra, owned by Mr. I. W. Everett.

and from kennels based on her stock. In 1987, she was named "Patron of the Irish Wolfhound."

Miss Noreen Twyman, a veterinarian and successful breeder and trainer of coursing Greyhounds, formed the Nendrum kennel and became a noted Irish Wolfhound expert after World War II. Her very well-known Int. Ch.

BEHOLD THE WOLF SLAYER!
The Irish Wolfhound of years ago could easily go after and kill a wolf. While such hunting and capturing instincts have been long diminished, a small moving object will reawaken his fun of the chase.

Colin of Nendrum was out of Carol of Eaglescrag and Sheelagh Seale's Int. Ch. McGilligan of Ballykelly. Her hounds produced sound and balanced litters and played a big role in improving the breed.

Anthony Killykeen-Doyle of Killykeen came from a family that had been involved in Wolfhounds since the 1800s. He bred his first litter in 1959, mating Ballykelly Kilkenny of Killykeen to Finnigan of Ballykelly. Kilkenny's second litter was out of Ch. Diarmuid of Dunamaise. These matings produced quality puppies, some of which went abroad to stock new kennels.

Killykeen Roisin of Woodenbridge proved very popular and is still a strong influence in the Killykeen kennels today. Killykeen Mars, beloved in the breed in the 1980s, produced top-quality progeny, including the following champions: Killykeen Spellbound, Killykeen Wolfwitch (top-winning Wolfhound in 1991) and Killykeen McGilligan. Another champion, Killykeen Destiny (out of Killykeen Max), had four Hound Group wins and the famous litter of Owenmore champions that boasted Tony's Owenmore Kittiwake, a champion, multiple Group winner, three-time Best in Show winner and top-winning bitch of 1994. Other offspring of Killykeen Max are champions in American and Canadian lure coursing and obedience.

In the 1960s, Miss Elizabeth Murphy formed Carrokeel, devoting herself to the breed's improvement and consistency of type. Her beautiful champion, Carrokeel Cara, was a several-time winner of the Height and Soundness Cup and Best in Show winner at the 1974 breed championship show. Her purchase of Eng. Ch. Boroughbury Justice as show and stud dog brought English blood into Ireland's Wolfhounds and has had a major effect on the breed today. Miss Murphy has been president of the Irish Wolfhound Club of Ireland, director of the Irish Kennel Club and president

of the Federation of European Irish Wolfhound Clubs.

John and Kathleen Kelly of Nutstown met their first Wolfhound in 1960 and were immediately won over. Mating Malatown Lady with a champion male, Boroughbury Justice, the resulting bitch, Nutstown Queen, was their first homebred champion and the beginning of their kennel's great success. Mated to Ballykelly Errislannan Liam, her son Int. Ch. Nutstown Kin was the top-winning Wolfhound in Ireland and England in 1980 and in Ireland in 1981. The wonderfully successful Int. Ch. Chieftain of

Brian Boru, the mascot of the Irish Guards, was a well-known Wolfhound because of the many visitors to the castle where the guards were on duty.

Irish Wolfhound puppies from a prominent Irish kennel of yesteryear, circa the late 1920s.

Nutstown took Best in Show at the Kilkenny Championship Show when only 6-and-a-half months old, gaining his title at 19 months old. For three successive years, 1986, 1987 and 1988, he was the Irish Wolfhound Annual Champion. Another favorite Nutstown hound is Int. Ch. Capitan of Shantamon, multiple Group and Best in Show winner and Annual Champion in 1994 and 1995. He was named Pedigree Chum Top Sire for 1995 and his son, Saringas Mr. Micawber, was Top-Winning Puppy in Britain.

Gulliagh kennel, owned by Timothy and Marion Finney of North County Dublin, has maintained continuous breeding lines for the last 30 years. Nendrum, Eaglescrag and Sanctuary lines formed the foundation of their kennel, along with the subsequent introduction and mating of Int. Ch. Carrokeel Coilte, called "Merlin." Merlin, a wonderful hound with a great head and presence, enhanced future stock. Merlin's progeny, in fact, produced some of Britain and Ireland's best stock of hounds in the late 1980s and early 1990s. Int. Ch. Hydebeck Reginald Snuffson won Top-Winning Wolfhound in Britain for three consecutive years, including Best of Breed at Crufts in 1989. His winning counterpart in Ireland, Int. Ch. Culvercroft Benjamin of Gulliagh, was the Irish National Champion for the three years before 1990 and won Best of Breed at England's Crufts Centenary show in 1991 out of a field of 197 dogs. Although the kennel has introduced outcross blood in recent years, it maintains its goal of great heads, correct height and good shape and movement. Gulliagh takes pride in the longevity of their hounds, almost all of whom live over nine years.

Tony and Ger Redmond's Athcarne kennel began its success with Maeve, an impressive good-tempered bitch bred from Ballykelly stock. She produced the titled Athcarne Shiofa, who in turn produced champions, all possessing wonderful hunting and coursing skills. Breed fanciers applaud Tony Redmond for his work in Wolfhound rescue, an

The Irish Wolfhound possesses a harmonious balance of physical beauty, working ability and a sound, reliable temperament.

effort he pursues as conscientiously as he does sound breeding.

All of the fine kennels described have bred or continue to breed top Irish Wolfhounds. Their founders attempt, through selective breeding, care and dedication to their stock, to produce the same Wolfhound that was so eloquently spoken of centuries ago. The breed is fortunate to have so many Irish Wolfhound fanciers in its homeland and abroad, willing to work toward the common goal of a fit, healthy breed, sound in mind and body.

IRISH COAT-OF-ARMS

Wolfhounds were used by Irish chieftains in war as well as in the hunt. The coat-of-arms of early Irish kings was composed of the shamrock, the harp and the Irish Wolfhound, underneath which was written the motto: "Gentle when stroked, fierce when provoked."

Ch. Breac
O'Shawn of Eagle,
winning the
Hound Group at
Westminster in
1975, owner-
handled by
Samuel E. Ewing
III, under judge
Tom Stevenson.

THE IRISH WOLFHOUND IN THE UNITED STATES

By Gretchen Bernardi

Essential to the understanding of the Irish Wolfhound, its history and its makeup, is the story of Capt. George A. Graham and his work that brought the breed back from the edge of extinction. His efforts and the writings he left behind, including the standard of excellence which we use today with only very slight changes, contribute to the saga of this magnificent hound, wherever he is found today.

Although we know from ancient drawings and documents

Ch. Broughshane of Eagle, winning Best in Show at Ramapo Kennel Club in 1973, owner-handled by Samuel E. Ewing III. The judge was N. R. Groh. Broughshane was one of the top winning Hounds in the US in the early 1970s.

BEST DOG IN SHOW

that it is an ancient breed, we know very little about the breeding and care of the dogs from that time, because the idea of a "pet Irish Wolfhound" is a modern concept. The dogs were kept and bred for utilitarian reasons, so those that performed their jobs well were presumably bred from and admired. Beloved as they likely were by their noble owners, they were kept first and foremost for the work they did. So it is important not to date the breed's presence by competition or registrations.

It is surprising to realize, then, that two Irish Wolfhounds, Tiger and Lion, came to America in the mid-19th century, about the time that Capt. Graham was engaged in his intense breeding program. These two Wolfhounds went to Henry Hastings Sibley, the first

Ch. Wildisle Warlock, born April 1, 1973, by Ch. Wildisle Wizard of Id out of Ch. Mistimourne Wildisle Mirage, owned and bred by Jill Richards Bregy.

IRISH WOLFHOUND CLUB
50 TH ANNUAL
SPECIALTY SHOW
MAY 3&4 1979
BEST OF BREED
JUDGE
MRS. CARL MORDEN
PHOTO BY THACKER

governor of Minnesota, and a life-size portrait of Lion, painted in 1842, still hangs in the Sibley Museum in Mendota, Minnesota.

Like the ancient hounds, many Wolfhounds were sent to the United States from England and Ireland to perform the task for which they were bred, especially in the Western states. One publication from 1892 reports that a dog bred in England and sent to the "Rocky Mountains," killed 40 wolves in one winter.

Nonetheless, it is through exhibition and registrations that we can trace the early history of the American Irish Wolfhound. Bevis was owned by J. Lester Wallack of New York, active in the theater at the time. Bevis was bred in Ireland and brought here by Dion Boucicault, Esq., an actor and playwright, who presented the dog to Mr. Wallack as a gift. Bevis was the first Irish Wolfhound to be exhibited in the US and, fittingly, the breed's debut in the American show ring was at Westminster Kennel Club in New York in 1879. Surprisingly, that was the same year the Kennel

Club of England established classes for Irish Wolfhounds and saw the first entry at the Irish Kennel Club show.

But even before Bevis made his New York debut, Gen. Roger D. Williams was establishing the first breeding kennel for the breed named Rookwood, located in Lexington, Kentucky, based on the importation of four hounds from England, some directly from Capt. Graham. Registration and showing requirements were considerably different then and, in fact, some of the first champions were not registered. Because many of the Rookwood dogs were unregistered, being sold to ranchers and farmers as working hounds, we

cannot determine exactly how many litters were produced there. However, we do know that this kennel actually registered around 125 Wolfhounds and generated a great deal of interest in the breed.

By 1910, several people became interested in breeding and showing Irish Wolfhounds. B.F. Lewis, Jr. of Landsdowne, Pennsylvania imported several well-bred dogs from Ireland and England and bred several litters. Joseph A. McAleenan of Brooklyn, New York imported dogs from Ireland and bred several litters over the next few years. A bitch from one of those litters went to Mrs. Norwood Smith and was the foundation of Cragwood Irish Wolfhounds, established in California around 1920. The Cragwood Wolfhounds figure prominently in early American Wolfhound pedigrees, but, just as

Ch. Stoneybrook Konjur, born June 6, 1994, by Stoneybrook Kaos out of Ch. Stoneybrook Sorcier, owned and bred by Dr. Lynn Simon and Judith Simon.

PURE-BRED PURPOSE

Given the vast range of the world's 400 or so pure breeds of dog, it's fair to say that domestic dogs are the most versatile animal in the kingdom. From the tiny 1-pound lap dog to the 200-pound guard dog, dogs have adapted to every need and whim of their human masters. Humans have selectively bred dogs to alter physical attributes like size, color, leg length, mass and skull diameter in order to suit our own needs and fancies. Dogs serve humans not only as companions and guardians but also as hunters, exterminators, shepherds, rescuers, messengers, warriors, babysitters and more!

Ch. Fleetwind Magnum, born April 21, 1985, by Ch. Fleetwind Dan out of Ch. Seawing Tara, owned and bred by Lois Thomasson.

importantly, Mrs. Smith herself was one of the driving forces behind the formation of the Irish Wolfhound Club of America and, later, in the formation of the Irish Wolfhound Association of the West Coast in 1941.

The Irish Wolfhound was relatively well established in America by the 1920s, but it comes as no surprise that the breeding of this giant dog for companionship and exhibition only, as opposed to his hunting and flock-guarding capabilities, required resources of space and money that few could supply. Fortunately for the breed, there were enough people who admired them and who could afford to keep them in numbers sufficient to carry on breeding programs.

Ambleside was established in 1924 by Mr. and Mrs. L.O. Starbuck in Michigan, later in California, based on Cragwood lines. Mrs. Starbuck, known usually as Alma or "Mrs. Ambleside," was a powerful force in the Wolfhound world. Ch. King Lir of Ambleside, bred by the Starbucks and owned by Mrs. N.T. Bellinger, was the second Irish Wolfhound to win an all-breed Best in Show and the first American-bred Wolfhound to do so. His success was just one of many to follow, with Ambleside producing 60 American champions and 5 Canadian ones, in addition to tremendous success at national and regional specialties. The kennel registered around 500 hounds, more than any kennel in the world at the time, and these dogs formed the foundation stock for many of the most famous kennels to follow. Mrs. Starbuck's *The Complete Irish Wolfhound* was the first breed book, still read by many Wolfhound owners today.

Other kennels that made strong and important contributions to the breed, the Wolfhound world and our present-day hounds include Halcyon, Whippoorwill, Killybracken, Kihone and Edgecliff, Riverlawn and later, Eagle, Fleetwind, Wildisle, Fitzarran and many others. The Irish Wolfhound

Despite the breed's great size, the Irish Wolfhound is an athletic, robust dog that enjoys vigorous games. As hounds, these dogs are gregarious and fun-loving.

kennels breeding and showing today carry, for the most part, the genes of those early lines, a few of which are still active. Fortunately for all lovers of the breed in the US, and in the rest of the world where American dogs are very much admired, the list is a long and healthy one: Erinwood, Limerick, Stoneybrook (and its offshoot kennel, Rockhart), Carrickaneena, Brimstone, Redtop, Berwyck, Castlemaine, Caraglen and several others.

The United States was not so far behind in organizing clubs to promote the breeding and showing of Irish Wolfhounds either. The first club formed for that purpose was the Irish Wolfhound Club, formed in 1885 in Britain, through the efforts of Capt. Graham. The Irish Wolfhound Club of Ireland followed in 1925 and the Irish Wolfhound Club of America quickly followed in 1926.

THE WOLFHOUND AROUND THE WORLD

While always beloved in Ireland and Britain, the Irish Wolfhound today is popular all over the world. Scandinavia, Belgium, Italy, Switzerland, the Netherlands, Australia, New Zealand, South Africa, Mexico, the United States and Canada, as well as Russia, Poland, Japan and many other countries all boast breed clubs, sighthound clubs or an increased interest in this breed. National kennel clubs are good sources if you wish to contact breeders in these countries.

Some dogs can never get too close to the ones they love. A typical Irish Wolfhound stands higher than his fawning owner. Train your dog when he is young (and smaller than you!).

IRISH WOLFHOUND

ARE YOU A WOLFHOUND PERSON?

Life with the Irish Wolfhound requires commitment and companionship. Make no mistake about this great-sized aristocrat. Although very impressive in appearance, there is nothing aloof about the Wolfhound's personality. This is a breed whose life's desire is to be right by your side, at home or in the field. More goodwill ambassador than warrior, he will quickly show you why he is called a "gentle giant." This Irish charmer will give you his heart, asking nothing more than that you give him yours— and at least one good sprint each day to show off his speed, stamina and superb sight.

The original work of the Wolfhound was hunting wolves and other large game. The largest and tallest of the galloping hounds, he would race across difficult rocky terrain with remarkable power and swiftness, catching and shaking his prey to death. Few Wolfhounds today will be asked to hunt a wolf, but they still retain their favored role of the past—man's best friend by the hearth! While the Irish Wolfhound's commanding appearance is meant to demonstrate dignity and courage, his typical soft expression makes him lovable in both looks and personality. His tough, hard coat sheds lightly,

A LAMB IN DISGUISE

J. A. McAleenan, in an early 20th-century tribute to the breed, called the Irish Wolfhound "A giant in structure, a lamb in disposition, a lion in courage."

In general, Irish Wolfhounds get along well with other dogs although time with small dogs requires supervision.

"I've got a secret!" True pack dogs, Irish Wolfhounds typically enjoy the company of their breed.

repels rain and entangling undergrowth and includes shades of gray, brindle, red, black, fawn, pure white or any other color that appears in the Scottish Deerhound. His expressive face often appears to be smiling and, indeed, he probably is! With his basic good health and easy coat maintenance, his grooming routine involves only a quick daily brushing, toenail care and a bath as needed.

The virtues of the Irish Wolfhound are boundless—as is the praise of his admirers. While his early human companions valued his courage during the hunt or in battle, today the Wolfhound's love of family and sensitivity to human moods make him an ideal family dog, adaptable to any owner who respects the needs of an energetic giant. However, don't forget his origins as a hunter! The innate instincts that characterize a sighthound may lead him on a merry chase of animals hardly considered "game." Small pet dogs and cats might well intrigue him in the city, while sheep or other livestock could tempt him in the countryside. You would do well to understand his special needs before assuming responsibility for this very large hunting dog.

This adaptable breed has an affinity for the young and an instinctive rapport with the old and handicapped. Obviously, small children should be instructed to treat their Wolfhound companion with kindness and respect, just as inactive

TRAINING BENEFITS

A shy Wolfhound may gain important confidence-building skills in obedience training. Likewise, a dominant pup may learn to channel his energies and eagerly look to you for leadership. Both temperaments require patience and positive challenges.

or older owners need to address the breed's size, strength, natural exuberance and need for exercise. The adolescent years particularly will challenge the owner as the Wolfhound goes through his clumsy, seemingly endless high-energy stage.

While the breed shows deep devotion to its family, don't be surprised if your Wolfhound appears aloof with strangers. Most Wolfhounds prefer to introduce themselves on their own terms, after a good sniff and assessment. And don't let his size and power persuade you that your hound is the perfect guard dog. Ironically,

One look into the Wolfhound's deep, expressive eyes and smiling face tells volumes about his friendly lovable nature and boundless devotion.

DELTA SOCIETY

The human-animal bond propels the work of the Delta Society, striving to improve the lives of people and animals. The Pet Partners Program proves that the lives of people and dogs are inextricably linked. The Pet Partners Program, a national registry, trains and screens volunteers for pet therapy in hospices, nursing homes, schools and rehabilitation centers. Dog-and-handler teams of Pet Partners volunteer in all 50 states, with nearly 7,000 teams making visits annually. About 900,000 patients, residents and students receive assistance each year. If you and your dog are interested in becoming Pet Partners, contact the Delta Society online at www.deltasociety.org.

though the breed has a deep and resounding voice, an Irish Wolfhound rarely barks! On the other hand, a stranger need only take in this giant's hard stare, poised posture and throaty rumble to figure out that he should keep his distance. Your Irish companion has the gift of sniffing and sifting out your friends versus your enemies, and you would do well to trust his instincts. Breeder, historian and Irish Wolfhound judge Linda Gover perhaps puts it best: "Their role in the family is as guardian rather than guard dog."

Assured but not aggressive, the Irish Wolfhound is compatible with other dogs and enjoys a canine friend. In fact, many breeders who keep their hounds in pack environments marvel at their natural affection for each other. However, when selecting his playmates and considering a multiple-pet household, keep in mind your Wolfhound's predisposed instincts. Given his propensity for the chase, supervising play with any small dogs is strongly advised. If it's small and it moves, it's game! That cute Toy Poodle down the road may easily read as "hare" to your Wolfhound. Be vigilant and keep the peace with your neighbors.

The true Irish Wolfhound fancier will first tell you that this is an amazingly sensitive dog. Your hound wants nothing more than to learn your language, tune in to your needs and anticipate what makes you happy. Look into the eyes of an Irish Wolfhound and you will see the gratitude, wonder and joy he takes in being your special friend. His faith in you will never waver, and you will want to deserve that trust by providing him with a life of emotional happiness and well-being.

Your hound needs to be with you and cannot be left alone for hours on end. Leaving him all day leads to frustration and boredom, which can quickly result in unwanted "home redecorating" or perhaps "singing the blues" (or a sad Irish song) in a plaintive voice heard throughout the neighborhood. A Wolfhound should be kept in the home with his family. He may love the outdoors, but human contact is his reason for being. He will thrive mentally and physically only if by your side; this is not an outdoors-only or kennel dog.

In the home, give your Irish Wolfhound his own special chair or bed and you will be surprised at how little room he takes up. That is, of course, assuming your hound is not given access to all furniture. Many owners will

GENTLE GIANT

Don't be fooled by the great size and strength of the Irish Wolfhound. Despite his heritage and once-fierce reputation for hunting wolves, this giant among breeds takes to children like a mother hen! With his affinity for young or old, he will charm and entertain all members of the family.

admit that given the chance, the Wolfhound will happily claim any comfortable spot in the home. In view of the floor space a Wolfhound can take up when lounging, some owners believe that relinquishing the furniture is the lesser of two evils! Savvy owners also advise that you relocate any ornamental treasures to high ground, lest the exuberant sweep of a happy tail remove them for you.

Because this is a bright, energetic breed, training and supervised play are crucial to getting the best out of your relationship with your Irish Wolfhound. From the day you welcome him home, touch your Wolfhound frequently, gently playing with his feet and face, getting him used to being handled by family members. Cuddle him and enjoy some rough-and-tumble playtime as well. Play and handling are perfect opportunities to bond with your new dog; they also are stimulating for his mind and help to satisfy his need to run off energy. A busy Wolfhound is a happy, easier-to-live-with Wolfhound!

Like any other smart dog, the Irish Wolfhound will quickly decide "who is boss." While hound puppies are usually adaptable in accepting and adjusting to new situations, setting boundaries right at the beginning will give them reasonable guidelines to follow and make them eager to

HEART-HEALTHY
In this modern age of ever-improving cardio-care, no doctor or scientist can dispute the advantages of owning a dog to lower a person's risk of heart disease. Studies have proven that petting a dog, walking a dog and grooming a dog all show positive results toward lowering your blood pressure. The simple routine of exercising your dog—going outside with the dog and walking, jogging or playing catch—is heart-healthy in and of itself. If you are normally less active than your physician thinks you should be, adopting a dog may be a smart option to improve your own quality of life as well as that of another creature.

please you. It is much like raising a child—a relationship of mutual respect is key to building a strong bond. "No" means no. "Sit"

Two key ingredients to a Wolfhound's happiness: the comforts of home and the companionship of a favorite friend.

means sit. Now, please! Say it only once. If you say it 100 times, your dog will learn to wait until you've said it 99 times. Give the command and if your hound doesn't understand—or is being purposely obstinate—gently but firmly enforce it. Above all, do praise him highly and exuberantly for making the "right" decisions. A treat, toys, hugs—whatever he loves best is his reward for being a good dog.

Force is futile with an Irish Wolfhound. Positive reinforcement, not punishment, is the very best method of training this quick-witted giant. Obedience training is not simply a battle of wits or a challenge to see "who's in charge," it is the establishment of a lifetime companion relationship—and it may also save your Wolfhound's life. Responding quickly to a command such as "Drop it!" or "Down" has saved many dogs from poisoning or physical injuries on the street or in the field.

Perhaps the greatest bonus of having a trained Irish Wolfhound in your home is the delight of a canine companion who has learned the pleasure and rewards of pleasing you. Your companion is sharing your lifestyle; you are not adjusting to his personal whims. What new trainers and owners learn is that the dog is happier for knowing what is expected of him. The training relationship earns you his trust, respect and affection. The Wolfhound rarely snares a top placement at an obedience event, but don't let this clever giant fool you. He is perfectly trainable. His potential is limitless, and many Irish Wolfhounds have titles in various types of competition to prove it. Training brings out his best—his affection, courage and dignity. If he loves you, he will love to please you and will delight in a working partnership as much as you do.

That said, keeping your Wolfhound stimulated and busy is also the best way to keep him out

THE FAMILY HOUND

This giant sporting dog requires as much personal attention and affection as the tiniest toy-dog companion. An Irish Wolfhound's main purpose in life is to be with his people. He will insist, and rightfully deserves, to be an active participant in family life.

of trouble. Physically, the breed is strong, active and sound. Captain Graham, who worked a lifetime to ensure the survival of the breed, stated in his final article: "...a firm stand must be made against awarding prizes to hounds that are not absolutely sound, as the breed is essentially a galloping one and meant for rough as well as fast work, and therefore coat, soundness of limb and freedom of action must be insisted on." Taking responsibility for his exercise must be one of your most important considerations in choosing this hunting hound. Do you have access to the space he needs for at least one bounding run a day? A daily walk along the road will stimulate his natural curiosity, but to see real joy in your hound, you must let him do what he does best—gallop with the freedom and grace for which he was bred.

If you wish to see the full potential of the Irish Wolfhound, attend a lure-coursing event in your area. Coursing, a skill for which the Wolfhound was first bred, has been a sport enjoyed by man and hound down through the ages. Lure coursing was developed in the US, but has begun to flourish in Britain and on the Continent as well. Its purpose is to test the hunting skills of sighthounds and show off their instinctive desire to hunt by sight. As your hound chases an artificial lure, he is judged on enthusiasm,

RESCUE ME!
If you do not have the time or energy for a puppy, consider adopting an adult hound in need of a home available through Irish Wolfhound rescue programs. The grateful devotion you receive will be every bit as rewarding as raising a pup.

follow-through, agility, speed and endurance. The spectacle of these graceful, exuberant hounds in full flight is exciting, entertaining and pure fun for the dogs *and* for their human companions. It's a wonderful, sociable day in the country where you will meet fellow Wolfhound enthusiasts and see the breed at its best.

HEALTH CONSIDERATIONS FOR THE WOLFHOUND

The Irish Wolfhound's lifespan is never long enough for those who love him. While some bloodlines seem to live longer than others, the

Do You Know about Hip Dysplasia?

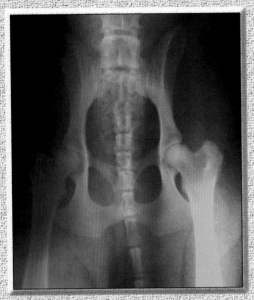

X-ray of a dog with "Good" hips.

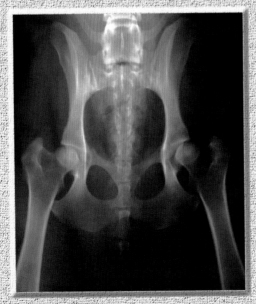

X-ray of a dog with "Moderate" dysplastic hips.

Hip dysplasia is a fairly common condition found in pure-bred dogs. When a dog has hip dysplasia, his hind leg has an incorrectly formed hip joint. By constant use of the hip joint, it becomes more and more loose, wears abnormally and may become arthritic.

Hip dysplasia can only be confirmed with an x-ray, but certain symptoms may indicate a problem. Your dog may have a hip dysplasia problem if he walks in a peculiar manner, hops instead of smoothly runs, uses his hind legs in unison (to keep the pressure off the weak joint), has trouble getting up from a prone position or always sits with both legs together on one side of his body.

As the dog matures, he may adapt well to life with a bad hip, but in a few years the arthritis develops and many dogs with hip dysplasia become crippled.

Hip dysplasia is considered an inherited disease and only can be diagnosed definitively by x-ray when the dog is two years old, although symptoms often appear earlier. Some experts claim that a special diet might help your puppy outgrow the bad hip, but the usual treatments are surgical. The removal of the pectineus muscle, the removal of the round part of the femur, reconstructing the pelvis and replacing the hip with an artificial one are all surgical interventions that are expensive, but they are usually very successful. Follow the advice of your veterinarian.

expected lifespan is about seven or eight years, with nine or ten considered a very long life. Your dog should be basically healthy throughout his life but, as in any breed, there are inherited diseases to watch out for. This list may seem daunting, but remember that most Wolfhounds are healthy dogs thanks to careful breeding. These diseases are presented not to scare, but to inform. Potential problems in the breed include: osteochondritis dissecans (OCD), a growth-related condition; hip dysplasia, a common condition in large-breed dogs causing a malformation of the hip joint; elbow dysplasia, a joint malformation disorder of the elbow; cardiomyopathy and other heart problems that can lead to death by heart failure; liver shunt; von Willebrand's disease, a defect of platelets that involves the clotting process; and progressive retinal atrophy (PRA), which leads to blindness. Bone cancer is also prevalent in the breed as well as lymphosarcoma, which is among the most frequently seen cancers in all dogs. Like other hereditary conditions, all of the aforementioned disorders can be prevented by not breeding dogs that are proven carriers.

Breeders also note that Wolfhounds, like most other sighthounds, are very sensitive to anesthetic; they require a great deal less than expected for their size and weight. When selecting your Irish Wolfhound's veterinarian, be sure to choose someone who is familiar with the special needs of both giant breeds and sighthounds. Discuss all of these issues with your vet from the outset.

One issue of which owners of deep-chested dogs like the Wolfhound especially must be aware is bloat, a term used to indicate gastric dilatation, gastric torsion (volvulus) or a combination of both. Air accumulates in

A NATURAL HUNTER

The Irish Wolfhound has a natural ability to hunt unassisted by man. Once he detects movement, his keen sight, breathtaking speed and enduring stamina take over, and the pursuit is exhilarating to watch. Many Wolfhound enthusiasts enjoy the sport of lure coursing—an opportunity to see their sighthounds in the chase for which they were bred.

the stomach (dilatation), usually caused by the dog's swallowing air. As the abdomen fills with air, it may twist on itself (torsion), obstructing the blood supply and preventing the exit of the air and stomach contents. This is very painful to the dog and, because the blood supply is compromised, shock and death of the stomach wall begins to occur quickly. Dilatation and torsion, whether occurring separately or together, are life-threatening and require immediate veterinary attention. Have an emergency vet's number handy and be ready to get there right away if you notice any of the symptoms, which include drooling, nausea, vomiting and retching, unproductive attempts to vomit or relieve himself, distended and/or hardened abdomen and general restlessness and inability to get comfortable. The risk of bloat can be greatly reduced by following simple daily precautions, discussed later in this book in the feeding and health sections.

The noble Irish Wolfhound seldom "complains" about discomfort; you will need to look into his eyes to detect signs of pain and illness. If he loses that merry, game gleam in the eye, you and your vet will need to determine the problem. Give him the best of care, attention and feeding, and add a generous dose of love. Assuming your Wolfhound is free of hereditary conditions, you will have the perfect prescription for a healthy and happy life.

ADDITIONAL PROBLEMS IN THE BREED

- **Bursas:** Many large-breed dogs, including the Wolfhound, develop swellings on the body at bony places (like the elbows) that come in contact with the floor when the dog lies down. The bursa actually is protecting the joint or bony area and is no cause for alarm unless infected. Soft bedding is good as treatment and as prevention. The bursas also can be bandaged with padding as they heal.
- **Hypothyroidism:** Underactivity of the thyroid, which is seen in many types of dog. If diagnosed, it is easy for the owner to manage at home with daily medication and dietary adjustments.
- **Megaesophagus:** A condition in which the esophagus weakens and becomes unable to transport of food; dilation of the esophagus along with loss of its muscle tone.
- **Fibrocartilaginous embolic myelopathy:** A condition most commonly seen in large-breed dogs in which pieces of cartilage enter a spinal artery or vein, causing obstruction of the blood supply and resulting in some degree of paralysis.
- **Seizures:** Seizures can affect all types of dog. They are sometimes epileptic but also can be caused by other factors such as sickness, trauma, environmental factors, etc.

Each breed recognized by the American Kennel Club has an approved standard that tells us what the breed should look like and what we should expect from its temperament. A good breeder works to produce dogs that meet this standard to assure that the breed you admire today will continue to thrive and improve in future generations. While the ever-elusive "perfect" dog will never be born, those devoted to the Irish Wolfhound work tirelessly to get as close to perfection as possible. Further, show judges use the standard to gauge the quality of the dogs in the ring.

Many breeders believe that to see an Irish Wolfhound truly meet the standard you must see him in his original work—galloping through rough terrain in pursuit of large game. In the Wolfhound, size is more than a measurement of height. Length and breadth, good bone and muscle must be proportionate to height. His movements should be easy and active, his head and neck carried high. The tail should be long and strong, carried with an upward

sweep, a "rudder" to steer and brake while in full flight.

As for temperament, a shy or fawning hound is said to lack the breed's desired commanding appearance. He may meet the standard in other ways, but unless his presence suggests a quiet dignity and sense of self, he will never be commanding of the attention and admiration that a Wolfhound deserves.

For those who cannot see the Irish Wolfhound in coursing action, dog shows are excellent opportunities to observe ideal examples of the breed. Not designed to be merely "beauty competitions," dog shows determine how closely each dog in the ring conforms to the ideal as described in the breed standard. Here you will see the Irish Wolfhound as close to perfection as today's breeders can produce, not only in soundness and appearance but also in attitude.

The descriptive Irish Wolfhound breed standard reflects the breeders' ideals and desire to perpetuate this gentle, aristocratic athlete through the generations.

Equipped with an understanding of this standard and an overall picture of the breed, the new owner can know what to expect from his Wolfhound and how to best meet his dog's special needs.

THE AMERICAN KENNEL CLUB BREED STANDARD FOR THE IRISH WOLFHOUND

General Appearance: Of great size and commanding appearance, the Irish Wolfhound is remarkable in combining power and swiftness with keen sight. The largest and tallest of the galloping hounds, in general type he is a rough-coated, Greyhound-like breed; very muscular, strong though gracefully built; movements easy and active; head and neck carried high, the tail carried with an upward sweep with a slight curve towards the extremity. The minimum height and weight of dogs should be 32 inches and 120 pounds; of

The temperament of the Irish Wolfhound, a dog that stands upward of 30 inches at the shoulder, is paramount in every breeding program. While the breed has "great size and commanding appearance," underneath lies a gentle and kind demeanor.

bitches, 30 inches and 105 pounds; these to apply only to hounds over 18 months of age. Anything below this should be debarred from competition. Great size, including height at shoulder and proportionate length of body, is the desideratum to be aimed at, and it is desired to firmly establish a race that shall average from 32 to 34 inches in dogs, showing the requisite power, activity, courage and symmetry.

Head: Long, the frontal bones of the forehead very slightly raised and very little indentation between the eyes. Skull, not too broad. Muzzle, long and moderately pointed. Ears, small and Greyhound-like in carriage.

Neck: Rather long, very strong and muscular, well arched, without dewlap or loose skin about the throat.

Chest: Very deep. Breast, wide.

Back: Rather long than short. Loins arched.

Tail: Long and slightly curved, of moderate thickness, and well covered with hair.

Belly: Well drawn up.

Forequarters: Shoulders, muscular, giving breadth of chest, set sloping. Elbows well under, neither turned inwards nor outwards.

Leg: Forearm muscular, and the whole leg strong and quite straight.

Hindquarters: Muscular thighs and second thigh long and strong as in the Greyhound, and hocks well let down and turning neither in nor out.

BETTER THAN THE AVERAGE DOG

Even though you may never show your dog, you should still read the breed standard. The breed standard tells you more than just physical specifications such as how tall your dog should be; it also describes how he should act, how he should move and what unique qualities make him the breed that he is. You are not investing money in a pure-bred dog so that you can own a dog that "sort of looks like" the breed you're purchasing. You want a typical, handsome representative of the breed, one that all of your friends and family and people you meet out in public will recognize as the breed you've so carefully selected and researched. If the parents of your prospective puppy bear little or no resemblance to the dog described in the breed standard, you should keep searching!

Ch. Aodh Harp of Eagle, top Hound in the US in 1984, also won the Irish Wolfhound Club of America national specialty that year, owner-handled by Sam Ewing under breed specialist judge Mrs. Kelly Fox.

Feet: Moderately large and round, neither turned inwards nor outwards. Toes, well arched and closed. Nails, very strong and curved.

Hair: Rough and hard on body, legs and head; especially wiry and long over eyes and underjaw.

Color and Markings: The recognized colors are gray, brindle, red, black, pure white, fawn or any other color that appears in the Deerhound.

Faults: Too light or heavy a head, too highly arched frontal bone; large ears and hanging flat to the face; short neck; full dewlap; too narrow or too broad a chest; sunken or hollow or quite straight back; bent forelegs; overbent fetlocks; twisted feet; spreading toes; too curly a tail; weak hindquarters and a general want of muscle; too short in body. Lips or nose liver-colored or lacking pigmentation.

List of Points in Order of Merit:
1. *Typical.* The Irish Wolfhound is a rough-coated Greyhound-like breed, the tallest of the coursing hounds and remarkable in combining power and swiftness.
2. *Great size* and commanding appearance.

3. Movements easy and active.
4. Head, long and level, carried high.
5. Forelegs, heavily boned, quite straight; elbows well set under.
6. Thighs long and muscular; second thighs, well muscled, stifles nicely bent.
7. Coat, rough and hard, especially wiry and long over eyes and under jaw.
8. Body, long, well-ribbed up, with ribs well sprung, and great breadth across hips.
9. Loins arched, belly well drawn up.
10. Ears, small, with Greyhound-like carriage.
11. Feet, moderately large and round; toes, close, well arched.

12. Neck, long, well arched and very strong.
13. Chest, very deep, moderately broad.
14. Shoulders, muscular, set sloping.
15. Tail, long and slightly curved.
16. Eyes, dark.

Note—The above in no way alters the "Standard of Excellence," which must in all cases be rigidly adhered to; they simply give the various points in order of merit. If in any case they appear at variance with Standard of Excellence, it is the latter which is correct.

Approved September 12, 1950

In 2000, Sam Ewing won the Breed at Westminster with the imported male Ch. Pitlochry's Grey Eagle.

Head, showing correct profile.

Faulty head due to short weak foreface, light eyes,
rounded topskull and large floppy ears.

6ft.

The Irish Wolfhound is a large hound; on his hindlegs, he is
easily the height of a 6-foot man.

Body with correct proportions and outline.

Faulty body due to long back, weak or "soft" topline, weak pasterns and rear.

Faulty body due to straight rear, upright shoulder, poor topline, lack of bone and substance and hooked tail.

IRISH WOLFHOUND

SELECTING YOUR PUPPY
Assuming you have done thorough research on the breed, including having gone to a couple of dog shows or coursing events and studying the Irish Wolfhound standard, and you have decided that you and the Wolfhound are a good match, you are ready to embark on the beginning of a very special relationship with a living, loving being. You should also expect to embark on a relationship with your dog's breeder. Choosing a Wolfhound means committing yourself to the care and training of a highly sensitive, people-loving active breed. A good breeder will and should scrutinize you to see if you are up to the responsibility of dog ownership. Just as you deserve a breeder with admirable ethics and the best possible reputation, the breeder needs to know that his puppy will have the family and the lifestyle for which he has been bred.

A loving relationship between owner and dog is all-important, but also of concern is how the dog will fit into your lifestyle. You will have to be confident that you have the time and willingness to meet the needs of a dog that requires the love of his human family even more than he needs his own kind. You must understand that this is a large and lively

FINDING A QUALIFIED BREEDER
Before you begin your puppy search, ask for references from your veterinarian, other breeders and other Wolfhound owners to refer you to someone they believe is reputable. Responsible breeders usually raise only one or two breeds of dog. Avoid any breeder who has several different breeds or has several litters at the same time. Dedicated breeders are usually involved with a breed or other dog club. Many participate in some sport or activity related to their breed. Just as you want to be assured of the breeder's qualifications, the breeder wants to be assured that you will make a worthy owner. Expect the breeder to interview you, asking questions about your goals for the pup, your experience with dogs and what kind of home you will provide.

dog that will need training as a puppy, and that his good-sized meals will make food bills a major budget consideration. Finally, you must appreciate that daily gallops are so important to satisfy the adult Wolfhound's instinct to run. Will you have access to a safely enclosed area in which to provide your Wolfhound his needed off-leash exercise? Once the breeder "selects" you, you will be grateful for the relationship. This is the person to whom you will turn over and over again with anxious questions, small calamities and joyful milestones.

The American Kennel Club-recognized parent club for the breed, the Irish Wolfhound Club of America, is a trusted source for referrals to breeders all over the country. Dog shows are also ideal places to observe the breed and to talk to breeders and handlers, who take great pride in their Wolfhounds and enjoy the chance to share their enthusiasm with interested newcomers. Please, however, visit with the Wolf-hound people only after they are finished competing. Showing a dog takes much preparation and concentration, and they will be able to spend time with you and answer your questions after the competition is over.

Above all, be prepared to wait for the breeder and dog you want. Good breeders often have waiting lists, but there is a reason

SIGNS OF A HEALTHY PUPPY
Healthy puppies are robust little fellows who are alert and active, sporting shiny coats and supple skin. They should not appear lethargic, bloated or pot-bellied, nor should they have flaky skin or runny or crusted eyes or noses. Their stools should be firm and well formed, with no evidence of blood or mucus.

for that—they have good dogs! The wait will be worth it. Don't rush into an impulse buy from a questionable breeder, as you will pay for it in dollars and heartache later.

Breeders commonly allow visitors to see the litter by around the fifth or sixth week, and puppies leave for their new homes around the eighth week. Puppies need to learn the rules of the pack from their dams, and most dams continue teaching the pups manners and dos and don'ts until around the eighth week. Breeders spend significant

Observe the littermates interacting with one another. It's more than enjoyable, it's educational to learn about each pup's temperament.

amounts of time with the Irish Wolfhound pups so that they are able to interact with the "other species" i.e., humans. Given the long history that dogs and humans have, bonding between the two species is natural but must be nurtured. A well-bred, well-socialized Irish Wolfhound pup wants nothing more than to be near you and please you.

Choosing from a litter is an eagerly anticipated, exciting and often emotional time. While the breeder should help you select the puppy that is best for you, it is wise to know some of the physical traits to look for. Most faults with which the puppy is born will not go away, so if physical conformation is important to you, for example if you aspire to show, make certain that the young puppy is free of faults. He should appear healthy, with a clean shiny coat and lively, alert eyes. Strong and straight limbs with no unusual bends or twists are important in this breed, as is a long, thick,

strong tail. Don't be surprised if the puppy's knees and feet are amusingly large, endearing traits at this stage. The Wolfhound's color is so varied that it's really a matter of your own preference. Your breeder will no doubt advise you that as the pup matures and the puppy coat is replaced, the shade may change and you may end up with a different-colored dog.

Temperament is, of course, what you and the breeder will be looking for in a companion, so it makes good sense to tap into the breeder's knowledge and intuition. The breeder has seen the litter interact and knows the bold puppy, scrambling for first dibs at human attention, and the more laid-back puppy, sweet but needing a little coaxing to join in the fun. Some breeders may express personal opinions on males versus

GETTING ACQUAINTED
When visiting a litter, ask the breeder for suggestions on how best to interact with the puppies. If possible, get right into the middle of the pack and sit down with them. Observe which pups climb into your lap and which ones shy away. Toss a toy for them to chase and bring back to you. It's easy to fall in love with the puppy who picks you, but keep your future objectives in mind before you make your final decision.

females. Some see their males as less independent and more trainable, and their females as clever but a bit less eager to please. All seem to agree that differences are slight and that each Wolfhound has a unique personality and approach to life. No one personality is right for all owners. The breeder can help you select the pup that will blend best into your own personal lifestyle.

If the breeder has the puppies' parents or relatives on the premises, you should see them as well as the litter. At the very least, the breeder will have the dam for you to meet (if he doesn't, this is a red flag!). Observing the pup's family will give you some idea of temperament and what you can expect when your puppy grows into an adult dog. Just as in people, physical and temperamental traits are passed on from generation to generation. Some parents produce attentive pups, eager to please. Others may pass along the traits of aloofness and independence.

Be sure to ask your breeder about the hereditary conditions seen in the breed and ask to see documentation of hereditary testing and health clearances on the parents of the litter and, where applicable, the puppies. Important clearances come from the Orthopedic Foundation for Animals (OFA), which tests for orthopedic and other hereditary

THE FAMILY TREE

Your puppy's pedigree is his family tree. Just as a child may resemble his parents and grandparents, so too will a puppy reflect the qualities, good and bad, of his ancestors, especially those in the first two generations. Therefore it's important to know as much as possible about a puppy's immediate relatives. Reputable and experienced breeders should be able to explain the pedigree and why they chose to breed from the particular dogs they used.

problems, and the Canine Eye Registration Foundation (CERF) for hereditary eye disease. Longevity and health are all-important in selecting a Wolfhound.

The devoted Irish Wolfhound breeders you visit have worked diligently to produce well-bred, well-socialized puppies. Now their hope is to provide them with

SELECTING FROM THE LITTER

Before you visit a litter of puppies, promise yourself that you won't fall for the first pretty face you see! Decide on your goals for your puppy—show prospect, lure-coursing dog, obedience competitor, family companion—and then look for a puppy who displays the appropriate qualities. In most litters, there is an alpha pup (the bossy puppy), and occasionally a shy fellow who is less confident, with the rest of the litter falling somewhere in the middle. "Middle-of-the-roaders" are safe bets for most families and novice competitors.

the best possible lives. When a breeder picks you to take home one of his puppies, you have all of his blessings and support, and you should look forward to a lifetime of mentoring and friendship.

COMMITMENT OF OWNERSHIP
You have chosen the noble Irish Wolfhound as the breed with which you want to share your life. This means that you have decided that the characteristics of the Wolfhound and the requirements of the breed can fit comfortably into your family and lifestyle. If you have selected a breeder, you have gone a step further—you have done your research and found a responsible, conscientious person who breeds healthy and temperamentally sound Irish Wolfhounds.

A visit with the puppies and their breeder will be an education in itself. Breed research, breeder selection and puppy visitation are very important aspects of finding the puppy of your dreams. Beyond that, these things also lay the foundation for a successful future with your pup. The breeder's experience in rearing Irish Wolfhound pups and matching their temperaments with appropriate humans offers the best assurance that your pup will meet your needs and expectations. The type of puppy that you select is almost as important as your decision that the Irish Wolfhound is the breed for you.

The decision to live with a Irish Wolfhound is a serious commitment and not one to be taken lightly. This puppy is a living sentient being that will be dependent on you for basic survival for his entire life. Beyond the basics of survival—food, water, shelter and protection—he needs much, much more. The new pup needs love, nurturing and a proper canine education to mold him into a responsible, well-behaved canine citizen. Your Irish Wolfhound's health and good manners will need consistent monitoring and regular "tune-ups," so your job as a responsible dog owner will be ongoing throughout every stage of his life. If you are not prepared to accept these responsibilities and commit to them for the next decade, likely longer, then you are not prepared to own a dog of any breed.

Everything about the Wolfhound is giant, including the commitment required in owning

A smooch for a sibling. Wolfhound littermates play, eat, sleep and learn together, forming a bond as part of their puppy pack.

one. Since the breed bonds so closely to his family, he does not transfer well if you decide later on that you cannot provide your dog with what a Wolfhound demands from his owners. For the sake of the puppy's life, make your choice wisely and confidently. There is no room in your Wolfhound pup's life for a near miss.

Although the responsibilities of owning a dog may at times tax your patience, the joy of living with your Irish Wolfhound far outweighs the workload, and a well-mannered adult dog is worth your time and effort. Before your very eyes, your new charge will grow up to be your most loyal friend, devoted to you unconditionally.

YOUR IRISH WOLFHOUND SHOPPING LIST

Just as expectant parents prepare a nursery for their baby, so should you ready your home for the arrival of your Irish Wolfhound

COST OF OWNERSHIP

The purchase price of your puppy is merely the first expense in the typical dog budget. Quality dog food, veterinary care (sickness and health maintenance), dog supplies and grooming costs will add up to big bucks every year. Can you adequately afford to support a canine addition to the family?

Observe the breeder's interactions with all of her dogs. The dogs' affection toward the breeder tells volumes about how she cares for them.

pup. If you have the necessary puppy supplies purchased and in place before he comes home, it will ease the puppy's transition from the warmth and familiarity of his mom and littermates to the brand-new environment of his new home and human family. You will be too busy to stock up and prepare your house after your pup comes home, that's for sure! Imagine how a pup must feel upon being transported to a strange new place. It's up to you to comfort him and to let your little pup know that he is going to be happy with you.

FOOD AND WATER BOWLS

Your puppy will need separate bowls for his food and water. Stainless steel pans are generally preferred over plastic bowls since they sterilize better and pups are less inclined to chew on the metal. Heavy-duty ceramic bowls are popular, but consider how often you will have to pick up those heavy bowls. Buy adult-sized pans, as your puppy will grow into them before you know it.

THE DOG CRATE

If you think that crates are tools of punishment and confinement for when a dog has misbehaved, think again. Most breeders and almost all trainers recommend a crate as the preferred house-training aid as well as for all-around puppy training and safety. Because dogs are natural den creatures that prefer cave-like environments, the benefits of crate use are many. The crate provides the puppy with his very own "safe house," a cozy place to sleep, take a break or seek comfort with a favorite toy; a travel aid to house your dog when on the road, at motels or at the vet's office; a training aid to help teach your puppy proper toileting habits; a place of solitude when non-dog people happen to drop by and don't want a lively puppy—or even a well-behaved adult dog—saying hello or begging for their attention. Breeders do not feel that it is suitable to crate a Wolfhound for long periods (e.g., while you are at work all day), but the crate can be helpful in many instances, especially housebreaking.

Crates come in several types, although the wire crate and the fiberglass airline-type crate are the most popular. Both are safe and your puppy will adjust to either one, so the choice is up to you.

The wire crates offer better visibility for the pup as well as better ventilation. Many of the wire crates easily fold down into suitcase-size carriers. The fiberglass crates, similar to those used by the airlines for animal transport, are sturdier and more den-like. However, the fiberglass crates do not fold down and are less ventilated than a wire crate, which can be problematic in hot weather. Some of the newer crates are made of heavy plastic mesh; they are very lightweight and fold up into slim-line suitcases. However, a mesh crate might not be suitable for a pup with manic chewing habits nor is it a good choice for a large-breed adult.

Don't bother with a puppy-sized crate. Although your Irish Wolfhound will be a wee fellow when you bring him home, he will grow by leaps and bounds, seemingly right before your eyes, and your puppy crate will be useless. Purchase a crate that will accommodate an adult Irish Wolfhound; the largest size available will be necessary. For the puppy, such a large crate can be partitioned with removable divider panels and his area

PEDIGREE VS. REGISTRATION CERTIFICATE

Too often new owners are confused between these two important documents. Your puppy's pedigree, essentially a family tree, is a written record of a dog's genealogy of three generations or more. The pedigree will show you the names as well as performance titles of all dogs in your pup's background. Your breeder must provide you with a registration application, with his part properly filled out. You must complete the application and send it to the AKC with the proper fee. Every puppy must come from a litter that has been AKC-registered by the breeder, born in the US and from a sire and dam that are also registered with the AKC.

The seller must provide you with complete records to identify the puppy. The AKC requires that the seller provide the buyer with the following: breed; sex, color and markings; date of birth; litter number (when available); names and registration numbers of the parents; breeder's name; and date sold or delivered.

Family-style dining for a hungry Wolfhound litter! The breeder starts the litter off on solid food as part of the weaning process.

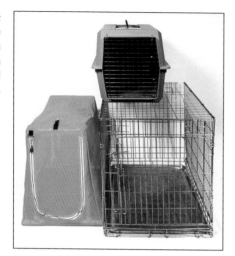

The three most common crate types: mesh on the left, wire on the right and fiberglass on top.

pads and other dog beds run the gamut from inexpensive to high-end doggie-designer styles, but don't splurge on the good stuff until you are sure that your puppy is reliable and won't tear it up or make a mess on it.

PUPPY TOYS

Just as infants and older children require objects to stimulate their minds and bodies, puppies need toys to entertain their curious brains, wiggly paws and achy teeth. A fun array of safe doggie toys will help satisfy your puppy's chewing instincts and distract him from gnawing on the leg of your antique chair or your new leather sofa. Most puppy toys are cute and look as if they would be a lot of fun, but not all are

expanded as he grows. A too-large area will not help him with house-training, nor will it make the pup feel as if he is in his own cozy den. Be aware that your pet-supply store may have to special-order an extra-large crate, so check into this well in advance of your pup's arrival home.

BEDDING AND CRATE PADS

Your puppy will enjoy some type of soft bedding in his "room" (the crate), something he can snuggle into to feel cozy and secure. Old towels or blankets are good choices for a young pup, since he may (and probably will) have a toileting accident or two in the crate or decide to chew on the bedding material. Once he is fully trained and out of the early chewing stage, you can replace the puppy bedding with a perma-nent crate pad if you prefer. Crate

CRATE EXPECTATIONS

To make the crate more inviting to your puppy, you can offer his first meal or two inside the crate, always keeping the crate door open so that he does not feel confined. Keep a favorite toy or two in the crate for him to play with while inside. You can also cover the crate at night with a lightweight sheet to make it more den-like and remove the stimuli of household activity. Never put him into his crate as punishment or as you are scolding him, since he will then associate his crate with negative situations and avoid going there.

necessarily safe or good for your puppy, so use caution when you go puppy-toy shopping.

Only the largest, sturdiest toys should be offered to an Irish Wolfhound pup or adult. The best "chewcifiers" are nylon and hard rubber bones, which are safe to gnaw on and come in sizes appropriate for all age groups and breeds. Be especially careful of natural bones, which can splinter or develop dangerous sharp edges; pups can easily swallow or choke on those bone splinters. Veterinarians often tell of surgical nightmares involving bits of splintered bone, because in addition to the danger of choking, the sharp pieces can damage the intestinal tract if swallowed.

Similarly, rawhide chews, while a favorite of most dogs and puppies, can be equally dangerous. Pieces of rawhide are easily swallowed after they get soft and gummy from chewing, and dogs have been known to choke on large pieces of ingested rawhide. Rawhide chews should be offered only when you can supervise the puppy.

When the Wolfhound is still a puppy, his adult-sized crate will be large enough for him to entertain company, though as he gets older there won't be much room left for guests.

Precious cargo! These littermates get a lift from a young friend.

Soft woolly toys are special puppy favorites. They come in a wide variety of cute shapes and sizes; some look like little stuffed animals. Puppies love to shake them up and toss them about, or simply carry them around. Be careful of fuzzy toys that have button eyes or noses that your pup could chew off and swallow, and make sure that he does not disembowel a squeaky toy to remove the squeaker! Braided rope toys are similar in that they are fun to chew and toss around, but they shred easily and the strings are easy to swallow. The strings are not digestible and, if the puppy doesn't pass them in his stool, he could end up at the vet's office. As with rawhides, your puppy should be closely monitored with rope toys.

If you believe that your pup has ingested a piece of one of his toys, check his stools for the next couple of days to see if he passes the item when he defecates. At the same time, also watch for signs of intestinal distress. A call to your veterinarian might be in order to get his advice and be on the safe side.

An all-time favorite toy for puppies (young and old!) is the empty gallon milk jug. Hard plastic juice containers—46 ounces or more—are also excellent. Such containers make lots of noise when they are batted about, and

Irish Wolfhounds love company and welcome the excitement of a crowd. These Wolfhound fanciers and their dogs are enjoying social time at a breed event.

puppies go crazy with delight as they play with them. However, they don't often last very long, so be sure to remove and replace them when they get chewed up.

A word of caution about homemade toys: be careful with your choices of non-traditional play objects. Never use old shoes or socks, since a puppy cannot distinguish between the old ones on which he's allowed to chew and the new ones in your closet that are strictly off limits. That principle applies to anything that resembles something that you don't want your puppy to chew.

COLLARS

A lightweight nylon collar is the best choice for a very young pup. Quick-clip collars are easy to put on and remove, and they can be adjusted as the puppy grows. Introduce him to his collar as soon as he comes home to get him

TOYS 'R SAFE

The vast array of tantalizing puppy toys is staggering. Stroll through any pet shop or pet-supply outlet and you will see that the choices can be overwhelming. However, not all dog toys are safe or sensible. Most very young puppies enjoy soft woolly toys that they can snuggle with and carry around. (You know they have outgrown them when they shred them up!) Avoid toys that have buttons, tabs or other enhancements that can be chewed off and swallowed. Soft toys that squeak are fun, but make sure your puppy does not disembowel the toy and remove (and swallow) the squeaker. Toys that rattle or make noise can excite a puppy, but they present the same danger as the squeaky kind and so require supervision. Hard rubber toys that bounce can also entertain a pup, but make sure that the toy is too big for your pup to swallow.

TOXIC PLANTS

Plants are natural puppy magnets, but many can be harmful, even fatal, if ingested by a puppy or adult dog. Scout your yard and home interior and remove any plants, bushes or flowers that could be even mildly dangerous. It could save your puppy's life. You can obtain a complete list of toxic plants from your veterinarian, at the public library or by looking online.

accustomed to wearing it. He'll get used to it quickly and won't mind a bit. Make sure that it is snug enough that it won't slip off, yet loose enough to be comfortable for the pup. You should be able to slip two fingers between the collar and his neck. Check the collar often, as puppies grow in spurts, and his collar can become too tight almost overnight.

LEASHES

A 6-foot nylon lead is an excellent choice for a young puppy. It is lightweight and not as tempting to chew as a leather lead. You can switch to a 6-foot leather lead after your pup has grown and is used to walking politely on a lead. For initial puppy walks and house-training purposes, you should invest in a shorter lead so that you have more control over the puppy. At first, you don't want him wandering too far away from you, and when taking him out for toileting you will want to keep him in the specific area chosen for his potty spot.

HOME SAFETY FOR YOUR PUPPY

The importance of puppy-proofing cannot be overstated. In addition to making your house comfortable for your Irish Wolfhound's arrival, you also must make sure that your house is safe for your puppy before you bring him home. There are countless hazards in the owner's personal living environment that a pup can sniff, chew, swallow or destroy. Many are obvious; others are not. Do a thorough advance house check to remove or rearrange those things that could hurt your puppy, keeping any potentially dangerous items out of areas to which he will have access.

Electrical cords are especially dangerous, since puppies view them as irresistible chew toys. Unplug and remove all exposed cords or fasten them beneath baseboards where the puppy cannot reach them. Veterinarians and firefighters can tell you horror stories about electrical burns and house fires that resulted from puppy-

If you do not want your Irish Wolfhound to lounge on the furniture as an adult, you will have to train him when he is a puppy. When an Irish Wolfhound sleeps on the sofa, he sleeps on the whole sofa!

chewed electrical cords. Consider this a most serious precaution for your puppy and the rest of your family.

Scout your home for tiny objects that might be seen at a pup's eye level. Keep medication bottles and cleaning supplies well out of reach, and do the same

THE GRASS IS ALWAYS GREENER

Must dog owners decide between their beloved canine pals and their perfectly manicured emerald-green lawns? Just as dog urine is no tonic for growing grass, lawn chemicals are extremely dangerous to your dog. Fertilizers, pesticides and herbicides pose real threats to canines and humans alike. Dogs should be kept off treated grounds for at least 24 hours following treatment. Consider some organic options for your lawn care, such as using a homemade compost or a natural fertilizer instead of a commercial chemical. Some dog-conscious lawnkeepers avoid fertilizers entirely, keeping up their lawns by watering, aerating, mowing and seeding frequently.

As always, dogs complicate the equation. Canines love grass. They roll in it, eat it and love to bury their noses in it—and then do their business in it! Grass can mean hours of feel-good, smell-good fun! In addition to the dangers of lawn-care chemicals, there's also the threat of burs, thorns and pebbles in the grass, not to mention the very common grass allergy. Many dogs develop an incurably itchy skin condition from grass, especially in the late summer when the world is in full bloom.

All puppies have an innate need to explore their surroundings, and they explore with their mouths. Be certain that all electrical cables are well out of the reach of your Wolfhound puppy or fastened tightly against the wall.

with waste baskets and other trash containers. It goes without saying that you should not use rodent poison or other toxic chemicals in any puppy area and that you must keep such containers safely locked up. You will be amazed at how many places a curious puppy can discover, especially a Wolfhound puppy who will grow tall very quickly and be able to reach higher and higher.

Once your house has cleared inspection, check your yard. A sturdy fence, well embedded into the ground, will give your dog a safe place to play and potty. An 8-foot-high fence is recommended to contain these agile sighthounds, who are always scanning the horizon and must see clear boundaries. Check the fence periodically for necessary repairs. If there is a weak link or space to squeeze through, you can be sure a determined Irish Wolfhound will discover it.

The garage and shed can be hazardous places for a pup, as

KEEP OUT OF REACH

Most dogs don't browse around your medicine cabinet, but accidents do happen! The drug acetaminophen, the active ingredient in certain popular over-the-counter pain relievers, can be deadly to dogs and cats if ingested in large quantities. Acetaminophen toxicity, caused by the dog's swallowing 15 to 20 tablets, can be manifested in abdominal pains within a day or two of ingestion, as well as liver damage. If you suspect your dog has swiped a bottle of pills, get the dog to the vet immediately so that the vet can induce vomiting and cleanse the dog's stomach.

A Dog-Safe Home

The dog-safety police are taking you on a house tour. Let's go room by room and see how safe your own home is for your new Irish Wolfhound. The following items are doggy dangers, so either they must be removed or the dog should be monitored or not have access to these areas.

Living Room

- house plants (some varieties are poisonous)
- fireplace or wood-burning stove
- paint on the walls (lead-based paint is toxic)
- lead drapery weights (toxic lead)
- lamps and electrical cords
- carpet cleaners or deodorizers

Outdoor

- swimming pool
- pesticides
- toxic plants
- lawn fertilizers

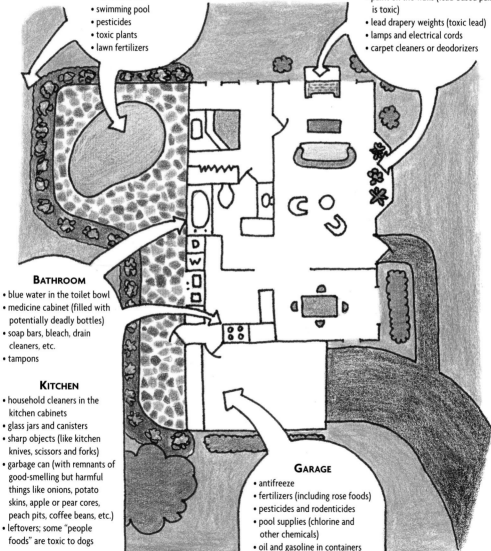

Bathroom

- blue water in the toilet bowl
- medicine cabinet (filled with potentially deadly bottles)
- soap bars, bleach, drain cleaners, etc.
- tampons

Kitchen

- household cleaners in the kitchen cabinets
- glass jars and canisters
- sharp objects (like kitchen knives, scissors and forks)
- garbage can (with remnants of good-smelling but harmful things like onions, potato skins, apple or pear cores, peach pits, coffee beans, etc.)
- leftovers; some "people foods" are toxic to dogs

Garage

- antifreeze
- fertilizers (including rose foods)
- pesticides and rodenticides
- pool supplies (chlorine and other chemicals)
- oil and gasoline in containers
- sharp objects, electrical cords and power tools

Monitoring your thirsty pup's water intake will aid in your house-training efforts, as you'll know when the pup needs to "go."

things like fertilizers, chemicals and tools are usually kept there. It's best to keep these areas off limits to the pup. Antifreeze is especially dangerous to dogs, as they find the taste appealing and it takes only a few licks from the driveway to kill a dog, puppy or adult, small breed or large.

VISITING THE VETERINARIAN

A good veterinarian is your Irish Wolfhound puppy's best health-insurance policy. If you do not already have a vet, ask friends and experienced dog people in your area for recommendations so that you can select a vet before you bring your Irish Wolfhound puppy home. It's preferable to find a vet who is experienced with giant breeds and sighthounds. Also arrange for your puppy's first veterinary examination before-hand, since many vets do not have appointments available immediately and your puppy

From his puppy shots to his senior-care program, your vet will be a true friend to your Irish Wolfhound throughout the dog's life.

should visit the vet within a day or so of coming home.

It's important to make sure that your puppy's first visit to the vet is a pleasant and positive one. The vet should take great care to befriend the pup and handle him gently to make their first meeting a positive experience. The vet will give the pup a thorough physical examination and set up a schedule for vaccinations and other necessary wellness visits. Be sure to show your vet any health and inoculation records, which you should have received from your breeder. Your vet is a great source of canine health information, so be sure to ask questions and take notes. Creating a health journal for your puppy will make a handy reference for his wellness and any future health problems that may arise.

MEETING THE FAMILY

Your Irish Wolfhound's homecoming is an exciting time for all members of the family, and it's only natural that everyone will

be eager to meet him, pet him and play with him. However, for the puppy's sake, it's best to make these initial family meetings as uneventful as possible so that the pup is not overwhelmed with too much too soon. Remember, he has just left his dam and his littermates and is away from the breeder's home for the first time. Despite his fuzzy wagging tail, he is still apprehensive and wondering where he is and who all these strange humans are. It's best to let him explore on his own and meet the family members as he feels comfortable. Let him investigate all the new smells, sights and sounds at his own pace. Children should be especially careful to not get overly excited, use loud voices or hug the pup too tightly. Be calm, gentle and affectionate, and be ready to comfort him if he appears frightened or uneasy.

Be sure to show your puppy his new crate during this first day home. Toss a treat or two inside the crate; if he associates the crate with food, he will associate the crate with good things. If he is comfortable with the crate, you can offer him his first meal inside it. Leave the door ajar so he can wander in and out as he chooses.

FIRST NIGHT IN HIS NEW HOME

So much has happened in your Irish Wolfhound puppy's first day

CONFINEMENT

It is wise to keep your puppy confined to a small "puppy-proofed" area of the house for his first few weeks at home. Gate or block off a space near the door he will use for outdoor potty trips. Expandable baby gates are useful to create puppy's designated area. If he is allowed to roam through the entire house or even only several rooms, it will be more difficult to house-train him.

away from the breeder. He's had his first car ride to his new home. He's met his new human family and perhaps the other family pets. He has explored his new house and yard, at least those places where he is to be allowed during his first weeks at home. He may have visited his new veterinarian. He has eaten his first meal or two away from his dam and littermates. Surely that's enough to tire out an eight-week-old Irish Wolfhound pup—or so you hope!

It's bedtime. During the day, the pup investigated his crate, which is his new den and sleeping space, so it is not entirely strange to him. Line the crate with a soft towel or blanket that he can snuggle into and gently place him into the crate for the night. Some breeders send home a piece of bedding from where the pup slept with his littermates, and those familiar scents are a great comfort for the puppy on his first night without his siblings.

He will probably whine or cry. The puppy is objecting to the confinement and the fact that he is alone for the first time. This can be a stressful time for you as well as for the pup. It's important that you remain strong and don't let the puppy out of his crate to comfort him. He will fall asleep

Consistency in your Irish Wolfhound's feeding schedule is important as a puppy and adult.

PUPPY PARASITES
Parasites are nasty little critters that live in or on your dog or puppy. Most puppies are born with ascarid roundworms, which are acquired from dormant ascarids residing in the dam. Other parasites can be acquired through contact with infected fecal matter. Take a stool sample to your vet for testing. He will prescribe a safe wormer to treat any parasites found in your puppy's stool. Always have a fecal test performed at your puppy's annual veterinary exam.

eventually. If you release him, the puppy will learn that crying means "out" and will continue that habit. You are laying the groundwork for future habits. Some breeders find that soft music can soothe a crying pup and help him get to sleep.

SOCIALIZING YOUR PUPPY
The first 20 weeks of your Irish Wolfhound puppy's life are the most important of his entire lifetime. A properly socialized puppy will grow up to be a confident and stable adult who will be a pleasure to live with and a welcome addition to the neighborhood.

The importance of socialization cannot be overemphasized. Research on canine behavior has proven that puppies who are not exposed to new sights, sounds, people and animals during their first 20 weeks of life will grow up to be timid and fearful, even aggressive, and unable to flourish outside of their home environment.

Socializing your puppy is not difficult and, in fact, will be a fun time for you both. Lead training goes hand in hand with socialization, so your puppy will be learning how to walk on a lead at the same time that he's meeting the neighborhood. Because the Irish Wolfhound is such a terrific breed, everyone will enjoy meeting "the new kid on the block." Take him for short walks, to the park and to other dog-friendly places where he will encounter new people, especially children. Puppies automatically recognize children as "little people" and are drawn to play with them. Just make sure that you supervise these meetings and that the children do not get too rough or encourage him to play too hard. An overzealous pup can often nip too hard, frightening the child and in turn making the puppy overly excited. A bad experience in puppyhood can impact a dog for life, so a pup that has a negative experience with a child may grow up to be shy or even aggressive around children.

Take your puppy along on your daily errands. Puppies are natural "people magnets," and most people who see your pup will want to pet him. All of these

encounters will help to mold him into a confident adult dog. Likewise, you will soon feel like a confident, responsible dog owner, rightly proud of your well-mannered Irish Wolfhound.

Be especially careful of your puppy's encounters and experiences during the eight-to-ten-week-old period, which is also called the "fear period." This is a serious imprinting period, and all contact during this time should be gentle and positive. A frightening or negative event could leave a permanent impression that could affect his future behavior if a similar situation arises.

Also make sure that your puppy has received his first and second rounds of vaccinations before you expose him to other dogs or bring him to places that other dogs may frequent. Avoid dog parks and other strange-dog

Interaction with littermates and the dam teaches the pups the limits of canine roughhousing. When a pup bites too hard, his playmates make it known.

areas until your vet assures you that your puppy is fully immunized and resistant to the diseases that can be passed between canines. Discuss safe socialization with your breeder and vet, as sometimes socializing the puppy even before he has received all of his inoculations is recommended.

LEADER OF THE PUPPY'S PACK

Like other canines, your puppy needs an authority figure, someone he can look up to and regard as the leader of his "pack." His first pack leader was his dam, who taught him to be polite and

not chew too hard on her ears or nip at her muzzle. He learned those same lessons from his littermates. If he played too rough, they cried in pain and stopped the game, which sent an important message to the rowdy puppy.

As puppies play together, they are also struggling to determine who will be the boss. Being pack animals, dogs need someone to be in charge. If a litter of puppies remained together beyond puppyhood, one of the pups would emerge as the strongest one, the one who calls the shots.

Once your puppy leaves the pack, he will look intuitively for a new leader. If he does not recognize you as that leader, he will try to assume that position for himself. Of course, it is hard to imagine your adorable Irish Wolfhound puppy trying to be in charge when he is still small and seemingly helpless. You must remember that these are natural canine instincts. Do not cave in and allow your pup to get the upper "paw"!

Just as socialization is so important during these first 20 weeks, so too is your puppy's early education. He was born without any bad habits. He does not know what is good or bad behavior. If he does things like nipping and digging, it's because he is having fun and doesn't know that humans consider these things as "bad." It's your job to teach him proper puppy manners, and this is the best time to accomplish that...before he has developed bad habits, since it is much more difficult to "unlearn" or correct unacceptable learned behavior than to teach good behavior from the start.

Make sure that all members of the family understand the importance of being consistent when training their new puppy. If you tell the puppy to stay off the sofa and your daughter allows him to cuddle on the couch to watch her favorite television show, your pup will be confused about what he is and is not allowed to do. Have a family conference before your pup comes home so that everyone understands the basic principles of puppy training and the rules you have set forth for the pup, and agrees to follow them.

The old saying that "an ounce of prevention is worth a pound of cure" is especially true when it

comes to puppies. It is much easier to prevent inappropriate behavior than it is to change it. It's also easier and less stressful for the pup, since it will keep discipline to a minimum and create a more positive learning environment for him. That, in turn, will also be easier on you.

SOLVING PUPPY PROBLEMS

CHEWING AND NIPPING

Nipping at fingers and toes is normal puppy behavior. Chewing is also the way that puppies investigate their surroundings. However, you will have to teach your puppy that chewing anything other than his toys is not acceptable. That won't happen overnight and at times puppy teeth will test your patience. However, if you allow nipping and chewing to continue, just think about the damage that a mature Irish Wolfhound can do with a full set of adult teeth.

Wolfhounds are sighthounds, and small animals can incite their need to chase. If raised with cats, Wolfhounds are typically good with them, but it's hard to make a generalization about the breed's behavior toward felines.

A teething pup loves soft toys, as chewing them relieves some pressure and pain of his aching gums.

Whenever your puppy nips your hand or fingers, cry out "Ouch!" in a loud voice, which should startle your puppy and stop him from nipping, even if only for a moment. Immediately distract him by offering a small treat or an appropriate toy for him to chew instead (which means having chew toys and puppy treats handy or in your pockets at all times). Praise him when he takes the toy and tell him what a good fellow he is. Praise is just as or even more important in puppy training as discipline and correction.

Puppies also tend to nip at children more often than adults, since they perceive little ones to be more vulnerable and more similar to their littermates. Teach your children appropriate responses to nipping behavior. If they are unable to handle it themselves, you may have to intervene. Puppy nips can be quite painful and a child's frightened reaction will only encourage a puppy to nip harder, which is a natural canine response. As with all other puppy situations, interaction between your Irish Wolfhound puppy and children should be supervised.

Chewing on objects, not just family members' fingers and ankles, is also normal canine behavior that can be especially tedious (for the owner, not the pup) during the teething period when the puppy's adult teeth are coming in. At this stage, chewing just plain feels good. Furniture legs and cabinet corners are common puppy favorites. Shoes and other personal items also taste pretty good to a pup.

The best solution is, once again, prevention. If you value something, keep it tucked away and out of reach. You can't hide your dining-room table in a closet, but you can try to deflect the chewing by applying a bitter product made just to deter dogs from chewing. Available in a spray or cream, this substance is vile-tasting, although safe for dogs, and most puppies will avoid the forbidden object after one tiny taste. You also can apply the product to your leather leash if the puppy tries to chew on his lead during leash-training sessions.

Keep a ready supply of safe chews handy to offer your Irish Wolfhound as a distraction when he starts to chew on something that's a "no-no." Remember, at this tender age he does not yet know what is permitted or forbidden, so you have to be "on call" every minute he's awake and on the prowl.

You may lose a treasure or two during puppy's growing-up period, and the furniture could sustain a nasty nick or two. These can be trying times, so be prepared for those inevitable accidents and comfort yourself in knowing that this too shall pass.

JUMPING UP

Pups of any breed can be notorious jumpers. Puppies jump up...on you, your guests, your counters and your furniture. Just another normal part of growing up, and one you need to meet head-on before it becomes an ingrained habit.

The key to jump correction is consistency. You cannot correct

THE FAMILY FELINE

A resident cat has feline squatter's rights. The cat will treat the newcomer (your puppy) as she sees fit, regardless of what you do or say. So it's best to let the two of them work things out on their own terms. Cats have a height advantage and will generally leap to higher ground to avoid direct contact with a rambunctious pup. Some will hiss and boldly swat at a pup who passes by or tries to reach the cat. Keep the puppy under control in the presence of the cat to help them become accustomed to each other.

Here's a hint: move the cat's litter box where the puppy can't get into it! It's best to do so well before the pup comes home so the cat is used to the new location.

This Wolfhound and his equine friend see just about eye to eye. Wolfhounds can be useful dogs to have on a farm and often get along well with all kinds of livestock as long as they are introduced and trained properly.

> ### DIGGING OUT
> Some dogs love to dig. Others wouldn't think of it. Digging is considered "self-rewarding behavior" because it's fun! Of all the digging solutions offered by the experts, most are only marginally successful and none is guaranteed to work. The best cure is prevention, which means removing the dog from the offending site when he digs as well as distracting him when you catch him digging so that he turns his attentions elsewhere. That means that you have to supervise your dog's yard time. An unsupervised digger can create havoc with your landscaping or, worse, run away!

Crate training has become a widely accepted training approach. The crate, when used properly, becomes the dog's "happy place" where he stays safe and out of mischief.

your Irish Wolfhound for jumping up on you today, then allow it to happen tomorrow by greeting him with hugs and kisses. As you have learned by now, consistency is critical to all puppy lessons.

For starters, try turning your back as soon as the puppy jumps. Jumping up is a means of gaining your attention and, if the pup can't see your face, he may get discouraged and learn that he loses eye contact with his beloved master when he jumps up.

Leash corrections also work, and most puppies respond well to a leash tug if they jump. Grasp the leash close to the puppy's collar and give a quick tug downward, using the command "Off." Do not use the word "Down," since "Down" is used to teach the puppy to lie down, which is a separate action that he will learn during his education in the basic commands. As soon as the puppy has backed off, tell him to sit and immediately praise him for doing so. This will take many repetitions and won't be accomplished quickly, so don't get discouraged or give up; you must be even more persistent than your puppy.

A second method used for jump correction is the spritzer bottle. Fill a spray bottle with water mixed with a bit of lemon juice or vinegar. As soon as puppy jumps, command him "Off" and spritz him with the water mixture. Of course, that means having the spray bottle handy whenever or wherever jumping usually happens.

Yet a third method to discourage jumping is grasping the puppy's paws and holding them gently but firmly until he struggles to get away. Wait a brief moment or two, then release his paws and give him a command to sit. He should eventually learn that jumping gets him into an uncomfortable predicament.

Children are major victims of puppy jumping, since puppies view little people as ready targets for jumping up as well as nipping. If your children (or their friends) are unable to dispense jump corrections, you will have to intervene and handle it for them.

Important to prevention is also knowing what you should not do. Never kick your Irish Wolfhound (for any reason, not just for jumping) or knock him in the chest with your knee. That maneuver could actually harm your puppy. Vets can tell you stories about puppies who suffered broken bones after being banged about when they jumped up.

Wolfhounds were born to please. With proper training and patience, your Wolfhound will develop into a reliable and welcome member of canine society.

"COUNTER SURFING"

What we like to call "counter surfing" is a normal extension of jumping and usually starts to happen as soon as a puppy realizes that he is big enough to stand on his hind legs and investigate the good stuff on the kitchen counter or the coffee table. Once again, you have to be there to prevent it! As soon as you see your Irish Wolfhound even start to raise himself up, startle him with a sharp "No!" or "Aaahh, aaahh!" If he succeeds and manages to get one or both paws on the forbidden surface, smack those paws gently and firmly tell him "Off!" As soon as he's back on all four paws, command him to sit and praise at once.

For surf prevention, make sure to keep any tempting treats or edibles out of reach (which means *way* up high or away in cabinets), where your Irish Wolfhound can't see or smell them. It's the old rule of prevention yet again.

PROPER CARE OF YOUR
IRISH WOLFHOUND

Discuss the proper feeding and nutrition of your Wolfhound with your breeder. Proper nutrition for such a large dog is crucial, and your breeder has the advantage of his experience in raising his own line of giant dogs.

FEEDING

Feeding your dog the best diet is based on various factors, including age, activity level, overall condition and size of breed. When you visit the breeder, he will share with you his advice about the proper diet for your dog based on his experience with the breed and the foods with which he has had success. Likewise, your vet will be a helpful source of advice throughout the dog's life and will aid you in planning a diet for optimal health.

FEEDING THE PUPPY

Of course, your pup's very first food will be his dam's milk. There may be special situations in which pups fail to nurse, necessitating that the breeder hand-feed them with a formula, but for the most part pups spend the first weeks of life nursing from their dam. The breeder weans the pups by gradually introducing solid foods and decreasing the milk meals. Pups may even start themselves off on the weaning process, albeit inadvertently, if they snatch bites from their mom's food bowl.

By the time the pups are ready for new homes, they are fully weaned and eating a good puppy food. As a new owner, you may be thinking, "Great! The breeder has taken care of the hard part." Not so fast.

A puppy's first year of life is the time when most of his growth and development takes place. This is a delicate time, especially for giant-breed pups like your Irish Wolfhound, and diet plays a huge role in proper skeletal and muscular formation. Improper diet and exercise habits can lead to damaging problems that will compromise the dog's health and movement for his entire life. With the myriad types of food formulated specifically for growing pups of different-sized breeds, dog-food manufacturers have taken much of the guesswork out of feeding. Growth-food formulas are designed to provide the nutrition that a growing puppy needs. Your breeder and vet can advise you of a good prepared food for the Wolfhound and will likely advise you how to add meat, vegetables and other natural components to the diet, as Wolfhounds fare better when fed some fresh foods. Research has shown that too much of certain vitamins and minerals predispose a dog to skeletal problems. It's by no means a case of "if a little is good, a lot is better," which is why you must take dietary advice from someone with experience. At every stage of your dog's life, not just in puppyhood, too much or too little in the way of nutrients can be harmful.

When you first bring your Wolfhound puppy home, the breeder will encourage you to continue feeding the pup what he has been fed up until then. Any changes to diet should be made gradually to avoid upsetting the puppy's digestion. Up to the age of 18 months, a young Wolfhound does well on four meals a day. Feedings can then be reduced to three meals a day, and then, at two years of age, to twice a day with the major meal given in the late evening so the dog can digest the meal while resting.

Regarding the feeding schedule, feeding the pup at the same times and in the same place each day is important for both housebreaking purposes and establishing the dog's everyday routine. As for

SWITCHING FOODS

There are certain times in a dog's life when it becomes necessary to switch his food; for example, from puppy to adult food and possibly from adult to senior-dog food. Additionally, you may decide to feed your pup a different type of food from what he received from the breeder, and there may be "emergency" situations in which you can't find your dog's normal brand and have to offer something else temporarily. Anytime a change is made, for whatever reason, the switch must be done gradually. You don't want to upset the dog's stomach or end up with a picky eater who refuses to eat something new. A tried-and-true approach is, over the course of about a week, to mix a little of the new food in with the old, increasing the proportion of new to old as the days progress. At the end of the week, you'll be feeding his regular portions of the new food, and he will barely notice the change.

NOT HUNGRY?

No dog in his right mind would turn down his dinner, would he? If you notice that your dog has lost interest in his food, there could be any number of causes. Dental problems are a common cause of appetite loss, one that is often overlooked. If your dog has a toothache, a loose tooth or sore gums from infection, chances are it doesn't feel so good to chew. Think about when you've had a toothache! If your dog does not approach the food bowl with his usual enthusiasm, look inside his mouth for signs of a problem. Whatever the cause, you'll want to consult your vet so that your chow hound can get back to his happy, hungry self as soon as possible.

the amount to feed, growing puppies generally need proportionately more food per body weight than their adult counterparts, but a pup should never be allowed to gain excess weight. Dogs of all ages should be kept in proper body condition, but extra weight can strain a pup's developing frame, causing skeletal problems.

Watch your pup's weight as he grows and, if the recommended amounts seem to be too much or too little for your pup, consult the vet about appropriate dietary changes. Keep in mind that treats, although small, can quickly add up throughout the day, contribut-

ing unnecessary calories. Treats are fine when used prudently; opt for dog treats specially formulated to be healthy or for nutritious snacks like small pieces of cheese or cooked chicken.

FEEDING THE ADULT DOG

With today's variety of nutritionally complete foods, choosing what you feed your Wolfhound should depend on what keeps your dog fit and what works best for you. To meet the nutritional needs of this active sighthound, balance is the key and should include proteins for muscle and speed, fats for energy (sighthounds thrive on high-fat diets), carbohydrates and vitamins and minerals. The latter two are already found in many prepared dog foods. If you prefer to feed your Wolfhound home-cooked food, and many breeders advise this, a diet containing a good supply of quality meat, cereal, wholemeal biscuit, cooked and raw vegetables, milk and eggs should meet nutritional standards.

Keep in mind, too, that dogs are essentially carnivores and your breeder may suggest feeding meat at least once a day. Protein affects speed and stamina and is crucial to the performance of your sighthound. To add a bit of variety to his diet, well-cooked rice or pasta should pique his interest and satisfy his body's need for carbohydrates. Also keep in mind

DIET DON'TS

- Got milk? Don't give it to your dog! Dogs cannot tolerate large quantities of cows' milk, as they do not have the enzymes to digest lactose.
- You may have heard of dog owners who add raw eggs to their dogs' food for a shiny coat or to make the food more palatable, but consumption of raw eggs too often can cause a deficiency of the vitamin biotin.
- Avoid feeding table scraps, as they will upset the balance of the dog's complete food. Additionally, fatty or highly seasoned foods can cause upset canine stomachs.
- Do not offer raw meat to your dog. Raw meat can contain parasites; it also is high in fat.
- Vitamin A toxicity in dogs can be caused by too much raw liver, especially if the dog already gets enough vitamin A in his balanced diet, which should be the case.
- Bones like chicken, pork chop and other soft bones are not suitable, as they easily splinter.

skin and coat. Of utmost importance, however, is that you do not attempt concocting a homemade diet for your Wolfhound without education and guidance from someone with experience. You must know how to deliver complete nutrition in proper proportions.

A "chow hound" but rarely a glutton, the Irish Wolfhound is often allowed, by his breeder, as much food as is desired at each meal. Because of his, oddly enough, small stomach, two smaller meals a day, morning and night, are preferred to one large meal. Multiple daily feedings are better for the dog's digestion and help protect him from deadly bloat (gastric torsion), which can result from a dog's eating too much at one time, among other causes. Along the same lines, do not feed or give water to a Wolfhound who has just come in

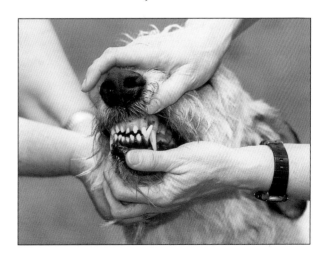

Crunchy food and treats are good for a dog's dental health, as the hard particles help scrape away plaque as the dog chews.

that certain "people foods," including chocolate, nuts, onions, grapes and raisins, are toxic to dogs and should never be given to a dog. Between-meal marrow bones or knucklebones are excellent for healthy teeth and gums, and a teaspoon of cod liver oil in the winter will do wonders for

A water bowl outside will help your Wolfhound quench his thirst. Just be careful to practice all bloat preventives regarding exercise, food and water.

As we feed our families and ourselves, feeding your Irish Wolfhound to ensure his fitness and health is basically a matter of common sense and knowing your own dog. Most Wolfhounds have healthy appetites and, as long as you meet his daily nutritional requirements, he will appreciate any added "creativity" in the dog dish. Second only to the sofa, the kitchen could well become your Wolfhound's favorite spot to spend time with you.

from strenuous exercise; wait at least an hour to feed him. Similarly, do not exercise your dog until at least an hour after mealtime. These are other important daily bloat preventives. Incidentally, while it once was advised to offer food and water in elevated bowls to bloat-prone dogs, there is now much debate about whether doing so can actually *increase* the risk of bloat. Discuss bloat and its preventive measures with your vet.

It may be hard to resist, but don't give in to a beggar! Rewarding his pleas encourages a habit that's both unhealthy and annoying.

FEEDING THE SENIOR DOG

A good rule of thumb is that once a dog has reached 75% of his expected lifespan, he has reached "senior citizen" or geriatric status. Your Irish Wolfhound will be considered a senior at about five years of age; based on his size, he has a projected lifespan of about seven to eight years. (The smallest breeds generally enjoy the longest lives and the largest breeds the shortest.)

What does aging have to do with your dog's diet? No, he won't get a discount at the local diner's early-bird special. Yes, he will require some dietary changes to accommodate the changes that come along with increased age. One change is that the older dog's dietary needs become more similar to that of a puppy. Specifically, dogs can metabolize more protein as youngsters and seniors than in the adult-maintenance stage.

Discuss with your vet whether you need to switch to a higher-protein or senior-formulated food or whether your current adult-dog food contains sufficient nutrition for the senior.

Watching the dog's weight remains essential, even more so in the senior stage. Older dogs are already more vulnerable to illness, and obesity only contributes to their susceptibility to problems. As the older dog becomes less active and, thus, exercises less, his regular portions may cause him to gain weight. At this point, you may consider decreasing his daily food intake or switching to a reduced-calorie food. As with all other changes, you should consult your vet for advice.

WATER

Just as your dog needs proper nutrition from his food, water is an essential "nutrient" as well. Be aware that Irish Wolfhounds are

WEIGHT AND SEE!

When you look at yourself in the mirror each day, you get very used to what you see! It's only when you pull out last year's vacation outfit and can't zip it that you notice that you've put on some pounds. Dog owners are the same way with their dogs. Often a few pounds go unnoticed, and it's not until some time passes or the vet remarks that your dog looks more than pleasantly plump that you realize what's happened. To avoid your pet's becoming obese right under your very nose, make a habit of routinely evaluating his condition with a hands-on test.

Can you feel, but not see, your dog's rib cage? Does your dog have a waist? His waist should be evident by touch and also visible from above and from the side. In top view, the dog's body should have an hourglass shape. These are indicators of good condition.

While it's not hard to spot an extremely skinny or overly rotund dog, it's the subtle changes that lead up to under- or overweight condition of which we must be aware. If your dog's ribs are visible, he is too thin. Conversely, if you can't feel the ribs under too much fat, and if there's no indication of a waistline, your dog is overweight. Both of these conditions require changes to the diet. A trip or sometimes just a call to the vet will help you modify your dog's feeding.

Wolfhounds are hungry around the clock, and there's not much that's out of his reach! "People food" can upset your Wolfhound's diet, add excess weight and even do serious harm.

TIPS FOR OUTDOOR SAFETY

Consider the following when encouraging your dog to get up and get moving in the great outdoors:

- The importance of water for your dog cannot be stressed enough. He needs a bowl of fresh clean water available, indoors and out. Dogs lose a lot of hydration when panting, and water is the only way to replace it.
- Children can be great playmates for dogs, but do not leave young children and dogs in the yard unattended. A dog can be overexcited by youngsters' boisterous play, causing him to act hyper or otherwise inappropriately.
- Your fenced yard must be a safe play place for your dog. Aside from making it escape-proof for him, keep it locked so that no one can let him out of the yard or enter without your knowledge.
- Never allow the dog to rush outdoors, possibly into danger. Have him sit/stay and wait for your command. If exiting into a non-fenced area, have him on lead. The dog will naturally follow the kids outside, so if the dog is to stay indoors, he should be put into his secure area before doors are opened.
- Limit your warm-weather exercise to the morning and evening hours when it's cooler, not the heat of midday.
- Keep your canine first-aid kit fully stocked and close at hand, along with emergency phone numbers.

notorious water drinkers, so, summer or winter, make certain that your Wolfhound has access to plenty of fresh water at all times, except at mealtimes. Water keeps the dog's body properly hydrated and promotes normal function of the body's systems. During house-training it is necessary to keep an eye on how much water your Irish Wolfhound is drinking, but once he is reliably trained he should have free access to clean fresh water. Make certain that the dog's water bowl is clean, and change the water often.

A word of caution concerning your deep-chested dog's water intake: he should never be allowed to gulp water, especially at mealtimes. In fact, he typically should not be given water at meal-times as a rule. This simple daily precaution can go a long way in protecting your dog from the dangerous and potentially fatal gastric torsion (bloat).

EXERCISE

As engaging and magnificent as this breed is, the prospective owner would do well to consider the freedom of space required by an athletic sighthound. Ownership of a large sporting dog entails ensuring that your hound's daily exercise needs are met. While a nice walk around the neighborhood will please him, he will never reach his full physical and mental soundness without an

PUPPY STEPS

Puppies are brimming with activity and enthusiasm. It seems that they can play all day and night without tiring, but don't overdo your puppy's exercise regimen. Easy does it for the puppy's first six to nine months. Keep walks brief and don't let the puppy engage in stressful jumping games. The puppy frame is delicate, and too much exercise during those critical growing months can cause injury to his bone structure, ligaments and musculature. Save his first jog for his first birthday!

exuberant off-leash sprint or two at least once a day. Galloping across the land is part of your Wolfhound's heritage and instinct. It is a thing of beauty to observe, and his pure joy and satisfaction after a good romp will keep him content for hours afterward. Of course, you must find securely enclosed, escape-proof areas for your Wolfhound's free exercise.

Much of the time your hound spends with you at home may be spent lounging on the family sofa or gazing contentedly from a large, safely fenced-in yard. As long as the area is adequate for him in which to play and have some fun, he should feel at home in his little "bit of kingdom." Of course, the Irish Wolfhound wants nothing more than to be with his family, so don't be surprised if he insists on joining you when you go inside. Exercise in the yard is only fun for him when you do it with him!

If you live in a city, don't despair about sharing your life with this hunting hound. A surprising number of Irish Wolfhounds can be found in major cities, comfortably ensconced in high-rise apartments. If your Wolfhound is given the proper daily exercise, he will thrive

almost anywhere. Many cities have nice-sized dog runs where your hound can zoom and bound about in a safely enclosed area with other canine companions. However, don't venture out to these canine playgrounds until you are certain that your dog is responsive to commands. Moreover, as with any off-lead dog, country or city dweller, you must ensure that he has an identification tag.

For those with the desire to see the beauty of the Irish

Proper nutrition and adequate exercise will be evident in your Wolfhound's overall good condition.

Wolfhound in full flight and to develop their hounds' natural instincts, there are lure-coursing events. Beyond the US, where these events started, they can be witnessed in Ireland, England, Germany, Canada and beyond. You can contact the Irish Wolfhound Club of America and sighthound organizations for details on how to get involved. Many owners also enjoy obedience competitions with their Wolfhounds. They take great pride in showing off the talents of a breed not always seen in the obedience ring. Keep your Irish Wolfhound fit and well exercised in mind and body and you will be rewarded with a happy, fulfilled companion.

GROOMING YOUR WOLFHOUND

BRUSHING

With a coat of good length and texture, it is not absolutely necessary to groom your Irish Wolfhound daily. But with his natural affinity for being by your side, if you accustom him to being brushed and handled, he will come to see grooming time as enjoyable and as an opportunity to spend time with you. You, in turn, will have a good-looking dog in prime coat condition. Grooming time will also give you the opportunity to examine your Wolfhound for any ear, eye or skin problems.

If your dog seems a bit hesitant or feisty at first, try alternat-

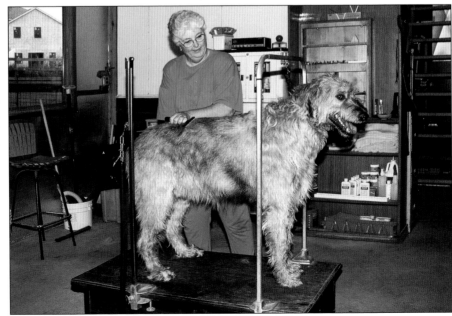

Using a grooming table is preferred by many owners. The table gives the handler more control over the dog, who accepts the table as a place to stand still and behave.

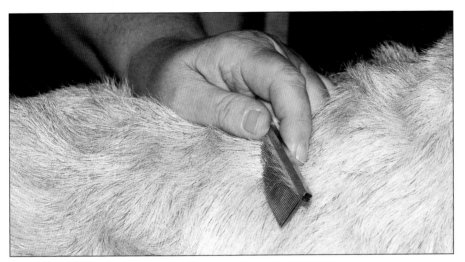

Combing through the Wolfhound's coat will keep it tangle-free. Make this a part of your regular grooming routine.

ing a little massage along with brushing, or give him an occasional treat as you groom. Within our human family, keeping a youngster clean and healthy expresses our love and concern for the child. It is the same for your dog. Your Wolfhound will appreciate the care you show him and see the experience as an expression of your love. Don't be surprised if he soon races over to you when you get out his brush!

Daily brushing will help remove dirt and dead hair and will stimulate your Wolfhound's natural skin oils, which are important in protecting him from the weather and promoting a coat with a healthy sheen. The tools you need are simple and easy to use. Practice makes perfect and you will be doing a good job in no time. Choose a fairly stiff bristle brush and a comb with spaced

teeth. If your hound's coat is particularly soft and long, a fine wire-toothed slicker brush or hound glove will do an equally good job.

Starting with the face and beard, very gently comb out any knots. Talk to your Wolfhound, reassuring him as you detangle his sensitive facial hair. Brush through and then move down the body, brushing smartly down the front, the sides of the shoulders, from neck to tail and underneath the body and legs. Carefully brush his tummy, and be sure to go down and in between each front and back leg. Don't forget the tail! Hair at the root and around the anus can become soiled and matted, so do inspect the area as part of your regular grooming routine. Brushing sessions should be a time of bonding for you and your

When shampooing, be sure to work the lather all the way down to the skin.

Wolfhound, and he should feel relaxed and content afterwards.

HAND STRIPPING

From time to time during the year, the coat of your Wolfhound can be improved with a little hand-stripping, which will get rid of dead hair, allow room for new hair growth and tidy up his appearance. While the show Wolfhound may require more artful tidying, "less is always more" with stripping and trimming. Start with your dog at an early age and you will both be "old pros" before you know it. Stripping, or plucking, is simply a matter of taking a few hairs between your finger and thumb and quickly pulling in the direction of growth. As with brushing, you can go from head to tail, accentuating the natural shape of your hound.

Don't be surprised if your dog has a "coat-casting" time of year, during which tufts of hair come out fast and furious. Encourage this with plucking and your Wolfhound soon will have a lovely new coat, perhaps even a shade darker or richer than before.

If you take your Irish Wolfhound to a professional groomer, do ask him to hand-strip your dog, as scissors or thinning shears can make the coat grow in too soft and thick, an incorrect texture for the breed. Remember— comb and pluck!

Unlike many other hounds, the Irish Wolfhound is, overall, a "self-cleaning" dog. His weather-resistant coat, kept in good condition, is practically odorless. Unless you show your hound, a couple of baths a year will probably keep him clean and easy to get close to! With good nutrition, exercise and a simple grooming routine, your Irish Wolfhound should look well, stay fit and grace your sofa for many years!

BATHING

Dogs do not need to be bathed as often as humans; in fact, as we've mentioned, bathing is necessary for the Irish Wolfhound only a couple of times each year for healthy skin and haircoat. Bathing may be necessary more often if your dog gets into something messy or if he starts to smell like a dog. Show dogs are usually bathed more frequently as well, although exactly how often depends on the owner. Bathing too frequently can have negative effects on the skin and coat, removing natural oils and causing dryness.

If you give your dog his first bath when he is young, he will become accustomed to the process. Wrestling a dog into the tub or chasing a freshly shampooed dog who has escaped from the bath will be no fun! Most dogs don't naturally enjoy their baths, but you at least want yours to cooperate with you.

Before bathing the dog, have the items you'll need close at hand. First, decide where you will bathe the dog. You should have a tub or basin with a non-slip surface. In warm weather, some like to use a portable pool in the yard, although you'll want to make sure your dog doesn't head for the nearest dirt pile following his bath! You will also need a hose or shower spray to wet the coat thoroughly, a shampoo formulated for dogs, absorbent towels and perhaps a blow dryer. Human shampoos are too harsh for dogs' coats and will dry them out.

Before wetting the dog, give him a brush-through to remove any dead hair, dirt and mats. Make sure he is at ease in the tub and have the water at a comfortable temperature. Begin bathing by wetting the coat all the way down to the skin. Massage in the sham-

Bathing an Irish Wolfhound is easy to do outside on a warm, sunny day. Your garden hose with a spray attachment will work nicely for a thorough rinse.

poo, keeping it away from his face and eyes. Rinse him thoroughly, again avoiding the eyes and ears, as you don't want to get water into the ear canals. A thorough rinsing is important, as shampoo residue is drying and itchy to the dog. After rinsing, wrap him in a towel to absorb the initial moisture. You can finish drying with either a towel or a blow dryer on low heat, held at a safe distance from the dog. You should keep the dog indoors and away from drafts until he is completely dry.

NAIL CLIPPING
Having his nails trimmed is not on many dogs' lists of favorite things to do. With this in mind, you will need to accustom your puppy to the procedure at a young age so that he will sit still (well,

Heavy-duty canine nail clippers will be needed for you to clip your Irish Wolfhound's nails at home.

on the clipping itself. The guillotine-type clipper is thought of by many as the easiest type to use; the nail tip is inserted into the opening, and blades on the top and bottom snip it off in one clip.

Start by grasping the pup's paw; a little pressure on the foot pad causes the nail to extend, making it easier to clip. Clip off a little at a time. If you can see the

as still as he can) for his pedicures. Long nails can cause the dog's feet to spread, which is not good for him; likewise, long nails can hurt if they unintentionally scratch, not good for you!

Some dogs' nails are worn down naturally by regular walking on hard surfaces, so the frequency with which you clip depends on your individual dog. Look at his nails from time to time and clip as needed; a good way to know when it's time for a trim is if you hear your dog clicking as he walks across the floor.

There are several types of nail clippers and even electric nail-grinding tools made for dogs; first we'll discuss using the clipper. To start, have your clipper ready and some doggie treats on hand. You want your pup to view his nail-clipping sessions in a positive light, and what better way to convince him than with food? You may want to enlist the help of an assistant to comfort the pup and offer treats as you concentrate

SCOOTING HIS BOTTOM

Here's a doggy problem that many owners tend to neglect. If your dog is scooting his rear end around the carpet, he probably is experiencing anal-sac impaction or blockage. The anal sacs are the two grape-sized glands on either side of the dog's vent. The dog cannot empty these glands, which become filled with a foul-smelling material. The dog may attempt to lick the area to relieve the pressure. He may also rub his anus on your walls, furniture or floors.

Don't neglect your dog's rear end during grooming sessions. By squeezing both sides of the anus with a soft cloth, you can express some of the material in the sacs. If the material is pasty and thick, you likely will need the assistance of a veterinarian. Vets know how to express the glands and can show you how to do it correctly without hurting the dog or spraying yourself with the unpleasant liquid.

"quick," which is a blood vessel that runs through each nail, you will know how much to trim, as you do not want to cut into the quick. On that note, if you do cut the quick, which will cause bleeding, you can stem the flow of blood with a styptic pencil or other clotting agent. If you mistakenly nip the quick, do not panic or fuss, as this will cause the pup to be afraid. Simply reassure the pup, stop the bleeding and move on to the next nail. Don't be discouraged; you will become a professional canine pedicurist with practice.

You may or may not be able to see the quick, so it's best to just clip off a small bit at a time. If you see a dark dot in the center of the nail, this is the quick and your cue to stop clipping. Tell the puppy he's a "good boy" and offer a piece of treat with each nail. You can also use nail-clipping time to examine the footpads, making sure that they are not dry and cracked and that nothing has become embedded in them.

The nail grinder, the second choice, is many owners' first choice. Accustoming the puppy to the sound of the grinder and sensation of the buzz presents fewer challenges than the clipper, and there's no chance of cutting through the quick. Use the grinder on a low setting and always talk soothingly to your dog. He won't mind his salon visit, and he'll have nicely polished nails as well.

EYE CARE

During grooming sessions, pay extra attention to the condition of your dog's eyes. If the area around the eyes is soiled or if tear staining has occurred, there are various cleaning agents made especially for this purpose. Look at the dog's eyes to make sure no debris has entered; dogs with large eyes and those who spend time outdoors are especially prone to this.

EAR CLEANING

The ears should be kept clean with a cotton wipe and ear powder made especially for dogs. Be on the lookout for any signs of infection or ear mite infestation. If your Irish Wolfhound has been shaking his head or scratching at his ears frequently, this usually indicates a problem. If his ears have an unusual odor, this is a sure sign of mite infestation or infection, and a signal to have his ears checked by the veterinarian.

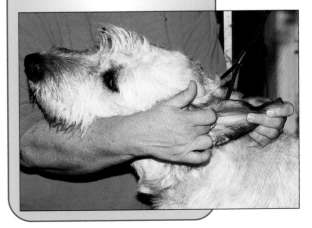

The signs of an eye infection are obvious: mucus, redness, puffiness, scabs or other signs of irritation. If your dog's eyes become infected, the vet will likely prescribe an antibiotic ointment for treatment. If you notice signs of more serious problems, such as opacities in the eye, which usually indicate cataracts, consult the vet at once. Taking time to pay attention to your dog's eyes will alert you in the early stages of any problem so that you can get your dog treatment as soon as possible. You could save your dog's sight!

IDENTIFICATION AND TRAVEL

ID FOR YOUR DOG
You love your Irish Wolfhound and want to keep him safe. Of course you take every precaution to prevent his escaping from the yard or becoming lost or stolen. You have a sturdy high fence and you always keep your dog on lead when out and about in public places. If your dog is not properly identified, however, you are overlooking a major aspect of his safety. We hope to never be in a situation where our dog is missing, but we should practice prevention in the unfortunate case that this happens; identification greatly increases the chances of your dog's being returned to you.

There are several ways to identify your dog. First, the traditional dog tag should be a staple in your dog's wardrobe, attached to his everyday collar. Tags can be made of sturdy plastic and various metals and should include

Two Wolfhounds and a small friend get ready to hit the road. For large dogs, many owners find it convenient to partition the back section of the vehicle to safely confine their dogs for travel.

your contact information so that a person who finds the dog can get in touch with you right away to arrange his return. Many people today enjoy the wide range of decorative tags available, so have fun and create a tag to match your dog's personality. Of course, it is important that the tag stays on the collar, so have a secure "O" ring attachment; you also can explore the type of tag that slides right onto the collar.

In addition to the ID tag, which every dog should wear even if identified by another method, two other forms of identification have become popular: microchipping and tattooing. In microchipping, a tiny scannable chip is painlessly inserted under the dog's skin. The number is registered to you so that, if your lost dog turns up at a clinic or

Whether traveling, exploring the neighborhood or just hanging out at home, your Irish Wolfhound should always be properly identified as a precautionary measure.

shelter, the chip can be scanned to retrieve your contact information.

The advantage of the microchip is that it is a permanent form of ID, but there are some factors to consider. Several different companies make microchips, and not all are compatible with the others' scanning devices. It's best to find a company with a universal microchip that can be read by scanners made by other companies as well. It won't do any good to have the dog chipped if the information cannot be retrieved. Also, not every humane society, shelter and clinic is equipped with a scanner, although more and more facilities are equipping themselves. In fact, many shelters microchip dogs that they adopt out to new homes.

In the US, there are five or six major microchip manufacturers as well as a few databases. The American Kennel Club's

PET OR STRAY?

Besides the obvious benefit of providing your contact information to whoever finds your lost dog, an ID tag makes your dog more approachable and more likely to be recovered. A strange dog wandering the neighborhood without a collar and tags will look like a stray, while the collar and tags indicate that the dog is someone's pet. Even if the ID tags become detached from the collar, the collar alone will make a person more likely to pick up the dog.

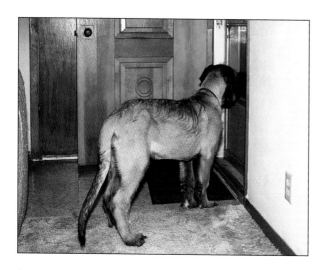

Companion Animal Recovery unit works in conjunction with HomeAgain™ Companion Animal Retrieval System (Schering-Plough). In the UK, The Kennel Club is affiliated with the National Pet Register, operated by Wood Green Animal Shelters.

Because the microchip is not visible to the eye, the dog must wear a tag that states that he is microchipped so that whoever picks him up will know to have him scanned. He of course also should have a tag with contact information in case his chip cannot be read. Humane societies and veterinary clinics offer microchipping service, which is usually very affordable.

Though less popular than microchipping, tattooing is another permanent method of ID for dogs. Most vets perform this service, and there are also clinics that perform dog tattooing. This is also an affordable procedure and one that will not cause much discomfort for the dog. It is best to put the tattoo in a visible area, such as the ear, to deter theft. It is sad to say that there are cases of dogs' being stolen and sold to research laboratories, but such laboratories will not accept tattooed dogs.

To ensure that the tattoo is effective in aiding your dog's return to you, the tattoo number must be registered with a national organization. That way, when someone finds a tattooed dog, a phone call to the registry will quickly match the dog with his owner.

DOGGONE!

Wendy Ballard is the editor and publisher of the *DogGone™* newsletter, which comes out bi-monthly and features fun articles by dog owners who love to travel with their dogs. The newsletter includes information about fun places to go with your dogs, including popular vacation spots, dog-friendly hotels, parks, campgrounds, resorts, etc., as well as interesting activities to do with your dog, such as flyball, agility and much more. You can subscribe to the publication by contacting the publisher at PO Box 651155, Vero Beach, FL 32965-1155.

ROAD TRAVEL

Car travel with your Irish Wolfhound may be limited to necessity only, such as trips to the vet, or you may bring your dog along almost everywhere you go. This will depend much on your individual dog and how he reacts to rides in the car. You can begin desensitizing your dog to car travel as a pup so that it's something that he's used to. Still, some dogs suffer from motion sickness. Your vet may prescribe a medication for this if trips in the car pose a problem for your dog. At the very least, you will need to get him to the vet, so he will need to tolerate these trips with the least amount of hassle possible.

Start taking your pup on short trips, maybe just around the block to start. If he is fine with short trips, lengthen your rides a little at a time. Start to take him on your errands or just for drives around town. By this time it will be easy to tell whether your dog is a born traveler or would prefer staying at home when you are on the road.

Of course, safety is a concern for dogs in the car. First, he must travel securely, not left loose to roam about the car where he could be injured or distract the driver. A young pup can be held by a passenger initially but should soon graduate to a travel crate, which can be the same crate he uses in the home. However, you must have a very large vehicle to accommodate your Wolfhound's crate, so you might fare better with another safety option. Other options include a car harness (like a seat belt for dogs) and partitioning the back of the car with a gate made for this purpose.

Bring along what you will need for the dog. He should wear his collar and ID tags, of course, and you should bring his leash, water (and food if a long trip) and clean-up materials for potty breaks and in case of motion sickness. Always keep your dog on his leash when you make stops, and never leave him alone in the car. Many a dog has died from the heat inside a closed car; this does not take much time at all. A dog left alone inside a car can also be a target for thieves.

Irish Wolfhounds are sociable, adaptable creatures who will enjoy accompanying you whenever they can.

TRAINING YOUR
IRISH WOLFHOUND

BASIC PRINCIPLES OF DOG TRAINING

1. Start training early. A young puppy is ready, willing and able.
2. Timing is your all-important tool. Praise at the exact time that the dog responds correctly. Pay close attention.
3. Patience is almost as important as timing!
4. Repeat! The same word has to mean the same thing every time.
5. In the beginning, praise all correct behavior verbally, along with treats and petting.

BASIC TRAINING PRINCIPLES: PUPPY VS. ADULT

There's a big difference between training an adult dog and training a young puppy. With a young puppy, everything is new. At eight to ten weeks of age, he will be experiencing many things, and he has nothing with which to compare these experiences. Up to this point, he has been with his dam and littermates, not one-on-one with people except in his interactions with his breeder and visitors to the litter.

When you first bring the puppy home, he is eager to please you. This means that he accepts doing things your way. During the next couple of months, he will absorb the basis of everything he needs to know for the rest of his life. This early age is even referred to as the "sponge" stage. After that, for the next 18 months, it's up to you to reinforce good manners by building on the foundation that you've established. Once your puppy is reliable in basic commands and behavior and has reached the appropriate age, you may gradually introduce him to some of the interesting sports, games and activities available to pet owners and their dogs.

Raising your puppy is a family affair. Each member of the family must know what rules to set forth for the puppy and how to use the same one-word commands to mean exactly the same thing every time. Even if yours is a large family, one person will soon be considered by the pup to be the leader, the alpha person in his pack, the "boss" who must be obeyed. Often that highly regarded person turns out to be the one who feeds the puppy. Food ranks very high on the puppy's list of important things! That's why your puppy is rewarded with small treats along with verbal praise when he responds to you correctly. As the puppy learns to do what you want him to do, the food rewards are gradually eliminated and only the praise remains. If you were to keep up with the food treats, you

TEACHER'S PET
Dogs are individuals, not robots, with many traits basic to their breed. Some, bred to work alone, are independent thinkers; others rely on you to call the shots. If you have enrolled in a training class, your instructor can offer alternative methods of training based on your individual dog's instincts and personality. You may benefit from using a different type of collar or switching to a class with different kinds of dogs.

could have two problems on your hands—an obese dog and a beggar.

Training begins the minute your Irish Wolfhound puppy steps through the doorway of your home, so don't make the mistake of putting the puppy on the floor and telling him by your actions to "Go for it! Run wild!" Even if this is your first puppy, you must act as if you know what you're doing: be the boss. An uncertain pup may be terrified to move, while a

Children and dogs that grow up together form a special bond of friendship.

bold one will be ready to take you at your word and start plotting to destroy the house! Before you collected your puppy, you decided where his own special place would be, and that's where to put him when you first arrive home. Give him a house tour after he has investigated his area and had a nap and a bathroom "pit stop."

It's worth mentioning here that if you've adopted an adult dog that is completely trained to your liking, lucky you! You're off the hook! However, if that dog

A dog the size of the Irish Wolfhound *must* be trained! It would be impossible to walk an adult Wolfhound who didn't know how to behave on leash.

spent his life up to this point in a kennel, or even in a good home but without any real training, be prepared to tackle the job ahead. A dog three years of age or older with no previous training cannot be blamed for not knowing what he was never taught. While the dog is trying to understand and learn your rules, at the same time he has to unlearn many of his previously self-taught habits and general view of the world.

> **KEEP IT SIMPLE—AND FUN**
> Practicing obedience is not a military drill. Keep your lessons simple, interesting and user-friendly. Fun breaks help you both. Spend two minutes or ten teaching your puppy, but practice only as long as your dog enjoys what he's doing and is focused on pleasing you. If he's bored or distracted, stop the training session after any correct response (always end on a high note!). After a few minutes of playtime, you can go back to "hitting the books."

Working with a professional trainer will speed up your progress with an adopted adult dog. You'll need patience, too. Some new rules may be close to impossible for the dog to accept. After all, he's been successful so far by doing everything his way! (Patience again.) He may agree with your instruction for a few days and then slip back into his old ways, so you must be just as consistent and understanding in your teaching as you would be with a puppy. (More patience needed yet again!) Your dog has to learn to pay attention to your voice, your family, the daily routine, new smells, new sounds and, in some cases, even a new climate.

One of the most important things to find out about a newly adopted adult dog is his reaction to children (yours and others), strangers and your friends, and how he acts upon meeting other dogs. If he was not socialized with dogs as a puppy, this could be a major problem. This does not mean that he's a "bad" dog, a vicious dog or an aggressive dog; rather, it means that he has no idea how to read another dog's body language. There's no way for him to tell whether the other dog is a friend or foe. Survival instinct takes over, telling him to attack first and ask questions later. This definitely calls for professional help and, even then, may not be a behavior that can be corrected 100% reliably (or even at all). If you have a puppy, this is why it is so very important to introduce your young puppy properly to other puppies and "dog-friendly" adult dogs.

BE UPSTANDING!

You are the dog's leader. During training, stand up straight so your dog looks up at you, and therefore up *to* you. Say the command words distinctly, in a clear, declarative tone of voice. (No barking!) Give rewards only as the correct response takes place (remember your timing!). Praise, smiles and treats are "rewards" used to positively reinforce correct responses. Don't repeat a mistake. Just change to another exercise—you will soon find success!

HOUSE-TRAINING YOUR IRISH WOLFHOUND

Dogs are tactility-oriented when it comes to house-training. In other words, they respond to the surface on which they are given approval to eliminate. The choice is yours (the dog's version is in parentheses): The lawn (including the neighbors' lawns)? A bare patch of earth under a tree (where people like to sit and relax in the summertime)? Concrete steps or patio (all sidewalks, garages and basement floors)? The curbside (watch out for cars)? A small area of crushed stone in a corner of the yard (mine!)? The latter is the best choice if you can manage it, because it will remain strictly for the dog's use and is easy to keep clean.

You can start out with paper-training indoors and switch over to an outdoor surface as the puppy matures and gains control over his need to eliminate. For the nay-sayers, don't worry—this

The dog/human bond is fostered early on through puppy socialization. A well-socialized, confident pup will be an easier pup to train.

won't mean that the dog will soil on every piece of newspaper lying around the house. You are training him to go outside, remember? Starting out by paper-training often is the only choice for a city dog.

WHEN YOUR PUPPY'S "GOT TO GO"
Your puppy's need to relieve himself is seemingly non-stop, but signs of improvement will be seen each week. From 8 to 10 weeks old, the puppy will have to be taken outside every time he wakes up, about 10–15 minutes after every meal and after every period of play—all day long, from first thing in the morning until his bedtime! That's a total of ten or more trips per day to teach the puppy where it's okay to relieve himself. With that schedule in mind, you can see that house-training a young puppy is not a part-time job. It requires someone to be home all day.

If that seems overwhelming or impossible, do a little planning. For example, plan to pick up your puppy at the start of a vacation period. If you can't get home in the middle of the day, plan to hire a dog-sitter or ask a neighbor to come over to take the pup outside, feed him his lunch and then take him out again about ten or so minutes after he's eaten. Also make arrangements with that or another person to be your "emergency" contact if you have to stay late on the job. Remind yourself—repeatedly—that this hectic schedule improves as the puppy gets older.

HOME WITHIN A HOME
Your Irish Wolfhound puppy needs to be confined to one secure, puppy-proof area when no one is able to watch his every move. Generally the kitchen is the place of choice because the floor is washable. Likewise, it's a busy family area that will accustom the

> ### MEALTIME
> Mealtime should be a peaceful time for your puppy. Do not put his food and water bowls in a high-traffic area in the house. For example, give him his own little corner of the kitchen where he can eat undisturbed and where he will not be underfoot. Do not allow small children or other family members to disturb the pup when he is eating.

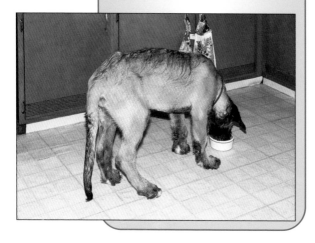

CANINE DEVELOPMENT SCHEDULE

It is important to understand how and at what age a puppy develops into adulthood.
If you are a puppy owner, consult this Canine Development Schedule to
determine the stage of development your puppy is currently experiencing.
This knowledge will help you as you work with the puppy in the weeks and months ahead.

PERIOD	AGE	CHARACTERISTICS
FIRST TO THIRD	BIRTH TO SEVEN WEEKS	Puppy needs food, sleep and warmth and responds to simple and gentle touching. Needs mother for security and disciplining. Needs littermates for learning and interacting with other dogs. Pup learns to function within a pack and learns pack order of dominance. Begin socializing pup with adults and children for short periods. Pup begins to become aware of his environment.
FOURTH	EIGHT TO TWELVE WEEKS	Brain is fully developed. Pup needs socializing with outside world. Remove from mother and littermates. Needs to change from canine pack to human pack. Human dominance necessary. Fear period occurs between 8 and 12 weeks. Avoid fright and pain.
FIFTH	THIRTEEN TO SIXTEEN WEEKS	Training and formal obedience should begin. Less association with other dogs, more with people, places, situations. Period will pass easily if you remember this is pup's change-to-adolescence time. Be firm and fair. Flight instinct prominent. Permissiveness and over-disciplining can do permanent damage. Praise for good behavior.
JUVENILE	FOUR TO EIGHT MONTHS	Another fear period about seven to eight months of age. It passes quickly, but be cautious of fright and pain. Sexual maturity reached. Dominant traits established. Dog should understand sit, down, come and stay by now.

NOTE: THESE ARE APPROXIMATE TIME FRAMES. ALLOW FOR INDIVIDUAL DIFFERENCES IN PUPPIES.

A big part of a dog's training is learning the house rules. A giant like the Wolfhound could easily clear off the table, so you must teach him from the outset that begging is unacceptable.

pup to a variety of noises, everything from pots and pans to the telephone, blender and dishwasher. He will also be enchanted by the smell of your cooking (and will never be critical when you burn something). An exercise pen (also called an "ex-pen," a puppy version of a playpen) within the room of choice is an excellent means of confinement for a young pup. He can see out and has a certain amount of space in which to run

SOMEBODY TO BLAME

House-training a puppy can be frustrating for the puppy and the owner alike. The puppy does not instinctively understand the difference between defecating on the pavement outside and on the ceramic tile in the kitchen. He is confused and frightened by his human's exuberant reactions to his natural urges. The owner, arguably the more intelligent of the duo, is also frustrated that he cannot convince his puppy to obey his commands and instructions.

In frustration, the owner may struggle with the temptation to discipline the puppy, scold him or even strike him on the rear end. Harsh corrections are unnecessary and inappropriate, serving to defeat your purpose in gaining your puppy's trust and respect. Don't blame your nine-week-old puppy. Blame yourself for not being 100% consistent in the puppy's lessons and routine. The lesson here is simple: try harder and your puppy will succeed.

about, but he is safe from dangerous things like electrical cords, heating units, trash baskets or open kitchen-supply cabinets. Place the pen where the puppy will not get a blast of heat or air conditioning.

In the pen, you can put a few toys, his bed (which can be his crate if the dimensions of pen and crate are compatible) and a few layers of newspaper in one small corner, just in case. A water bowl can be hung at a convenient height on the side of the ex-pen so it won't become a splashing pool for an innovative puppy. His food dish can go on the floor, next to but not under the water bowl.

Crates are something that pet owners are at last getting used to for their dogs. Wild or domestic canines have always preferred to sleep in den-like safe spots, and that is exactly what the crate provides. How often have you seen adult dogs that choose to sleep under a table or chair even though they have full run of the house? It's the den connection.

In your "happy" voice, use the word "Crate" every time you put the pup into his den. If he's new to a crate, toss in a small biscuit for him to chase the first few times. At night, after he's been outside, he should sleep in his crate. The crate may be kept in his designated area at night or, if you want to be sure to hear those wake-up yips in the morning, put

the crate in a corner of your bedroom. However, don't make any response whatsoever to whining or crying. If he's completely ignored, he'll settle down and get to sleep.

EXTRA! EXTRA!
The headlines read: "Puppy Piddles Here!" Breeders commonly use newspapers to line their whelping pens, so puppies learn to associate newspapers with relieving themselves. Do not use newspapers to line your pup's crate, as this will signal to your puppy that it is OK to urinate in his crate. If you choose to paper-train your puppy, you will layer newspapers on a section of the floor near the door he uses to go outside. You should encourage the puppy to use the papers to relieve himself, and bring him there whenever you see him getting ready to go. Little by little, you will reduce the size of the newspaper-covered area so that the puppy will learn to relieve himself "on the other side of the door."

parts, bits of stuffing or plastic or any other small pieces can cause intestinal blockage or possibly choking if swallowed.

PROGRESSING WITH POTTY-TRAINING

After you've taken your puppy out and he has relieved himself in the area you've selected, he can have some free time with the family as long as there is someone responsible for watching him. That doesn't mean just someone in the same room who is watching

Train your Wolfhound(s) to always use the same area of the property for bathroom duties. This makes for more convenient toileting as well as clean up.

Good bedding for a young puppy is an old folded bath towel or an old blanket, something that is easily washable and disposable if necessary ("accidents" will happen!). Never put newspaper in the puppy's crate. Also, those old ideas about adding a clock to replace his mother's heartbeat, or a hot-water bottle to replace her warmth, are just that—old ideas. The clock could drive the puppy nuts, and the hot-water bottle could end up as a very soggy waterbed! An extremely good breeder would have introduced your puppy to the crate by letting two pups sleep together for a couple of nights, followed by several nights alone. How thankful you will be if you found that breeder!

Safe toys in the pup's crate or area will keep him occupied, but monitor their condition closely. Discard any toys that show signs of being chewed to bits. Squeaky

LEASH TRAINING

House-training and leash training go hand in hand, literally. When taking your puppy outside to do his business, lead him there on his leash. Unless an emergency potty run is called for, do not whisk the puppy up into your arms and take him outside. If you have a fenced yard, you have the advantage of letting the puppy loose to go out, but it's better to put the dog on the leash and take him to his designated place in the yard until he is reliably house-trained. Taking the puppy for a walk is the best way to house-train a dog. The dog will associate the walk with his time to relieve himself, and the exercise of walking stimulates the dog's bowels and bladder. Dogs that are not trained to relieve themselves on a walk may hold it until they get back home, which of course defeats half the purpose of the walk.

TV or busy on the computer, but one person who is doing nothing other than keeping an eye on the pup, playing with him on the floor and helping him understand his position in the pack.

This first taste of freedom will let you begin to set the house rules. If you don't want the dog on the furniture, now is the time to prevent his first attempts to jump up onto the couch. The word to use in this case is "Off," not "Down." "Down" is the word you will use to teach the down position, which is something entirely different.

Most corrections at this stage come in the form of simply distracting the puppy. Instead of telling him "No" for "Don't chew the carpet," distract the chomping puppy with a toy and he'll forget about the carpet.

As you are playing with the pup, do not forget to watch him closely and pay attention to his body language. Whenever you see him begin to circle or sniff, take the puppy outside to relieve himself. If you are paper-training, put him back into his confined area on the newspapers. In either case, praise him as he eliminates while he actually is *in the act* of relieving himself. Three seconds after he has finished is too late! You'll be praising him for running toward you, or picking up a toy or whatever he may be doing at that moment, and that's not what you

DAILY SCHEDULE

How many relief trips does your puppy need per day? A puppy up to the age of 14 weeks will need to go outside about 8 to 12 times per day! You will have to take the pup out any time he starts sniffing around the floor or turning in small circles, as well as after naps, meals, games and lessons or whenever he's released from his crate. Once the puppy is 14 to 22 weeks of age, he will require only 6 to 8 relief trips. At the ages of 22 to 32 weeks, the puppy will require about 5 to 7 trips. Adult dogs typically require 4 relief trips per day, in the morning, afternoon, evening and late at night.

want to be praising him for. Timing is a vital tool in all dog training. Use it.

Remove soiled newspapers immediately and replace them with clean ones. You may want to take a small piece of soiled paper and place it in the middle of the new clean papers, as the scent will attract him to that spot when it's time to go again. That scent attraction is why it's so important to clean up any messes made in the house by using a product specially made to eliminate the odor of dog urine and droppings. Regular household cleansers won't do the trick. Pet shops sell the best pet deodorizers. Invest in the largest container you can find.

POTTY COMMAND

Most dogs love to please their masters; there are no bounds to what dogs will do to make their owners happy. The potty command is a good example of this theory. If toileting on command makes the master happy, then more power to him. Puppies will obligingly piddle if it really makes their keepers smile. Some owners can be creative about which word they will use to command their dogs to relieve themselves. Some popular choices are "Potty," "Tinkle," "Piddle," "Let's go," "Hurry up" and "Toilet." Give the command every time your puppy goes into position and the puppy will begin to associate his business with the command.

Scent attraction eventually will lead your pup to his chosen spot outdoors; this is the basis of outdoor training. When you take your puppy outside to relieve himself, use a one-word command such as "Outside" or "Go-potty" (that's one word to the puppy!) as you pick him up and attach his leash. Then put him down in his area. If he is too big for you to carry, snap the leash on quickly and lead him to his spot. Now comes the hard part—hard for you, that is. Just stand there until he urinates and defecates. Move him a few feet in one direction or another if he's just sitting there looking at you, but remember that this is neither playtime nor time for a walk. This is strictly a business trip! Then, as he circles and squats (remember your timing!), give him a quiet "Good dog" as praise. If you start to jump for joy, ecstatic over his performance, he'll do one of two things: either he will stop mid-stream, as it were, or he'll do it again for you—in the house—and expect you to be just as delighted!

Give him five minutes or so and, if he doesn't go in that time, take him back indoors to his confined area and try again in another ten minutes, or immediately if you see him sniffing and circling. By careful observation, you'll soon work out a successful schedule.

Accidents, by the way, are just that—accidents. Clean them up quickly and thoroughly, without comment, after the puppy has been taken outside to finish his business and then put back into his area or crate. If you witness an accident in progress, say "No!" in a stern voice and get the pup outdoors immediately. No punishment is needed. You and your puppy are just learning each other's language, and sometimes it's easy to miss a puppy's message. Chalk it up to experience and watch more closely from now on.

KEEPING THE PACK ORDERLY
Discipline is a form of training that brings order to life. For exam-

ple, military discipline is what allows the soldiers in an army to work as one. Discipline is a form of teaching and, in dogs, is the basis of how the successful pack operates. Each member knows his place in the pack and all respect the leader, or alpha dog. It is essential for your puppy that you establish this type of relationship, with you as the alpha, or leader. It is a form of social coexistence that all canines recognize and accept. Discipline, therefore, is never to be confused with punishment. When you teach your puppy how you want him to behave, and he behaves properly and you praise him for it, you are disciplining him with a form of positive reinforcement.

For a dog, rewards come in the form of praise, a smile, a cheerful tone of voice, a few friendly pats or a rub of the ears. Rewards are also small food treats. Obviously, that does not mean bits of regular dog food. Instead, treats are very small bits of special things like cheese or pieces of soft dog treats. The idea is to reward the dog with something very small that he can taste and swallow, providing instant positive reinforcement. If he has to take time to chew the treat, he will have forgotten what he did to earn it by the time he is finished!

Your puppy should never be physically punished. The displeasure shown on your face and in your voice is sufficient to signal to the pup that he has done something wrong. He wants to please everyone higher up on the social ladder, especially his leader, so a scowl and harsh voice will take care of the error.

TIME TO PLAY!

Playtime can happen both indoors and out. A young puppy is growing so rapidly that he needs sleep more than he needs a lot of physical exercise. Puppies get sufficient exercise on their own just through normal puppy activity. Monitor play with young children so you can remove the puppy when he's had enough, or calm the kids if they get too rowdy. Almost all puppies love to chase after a toy you've thrown, and you can turn your games into educational activities. Every time your puppy brings the toy back to you, say "Give it" (or "Drop it") followed by "Good dog" and throwing it again. If he's reluctant to give it to you, offer a small treat so that he drops the toy as he takes the treat. He will soon get the idea.

In addition to the basic obedience commands, show dogs must learn to stay in a standing position for examination by the judge.

Growling out the word "Shame!" when the pup is caught in the act of doing something wrong is better than the repetitive "No." Some dogs hear "No" so often that they begin to think it's their name! By the way, do not use the dog's name when you're correcting him. His name is reserved to get his attention for something pleasant about to take place.

There are punishments that have nothing to do with you. For example, your dog may think that chasing cats is one reason for his existence. You can try to stop it as much as you like but without success because it's such fun for the dog. But one good hissing, spitting swipe of a cat's claws across the dog's nose will put an

end to the game forever. Intervene only when your dog's eyeball is seriously at risk. Cat scratches can cause permanent damage to an innocent but annoying puppy.

PUPPY KINDERGARTEN

COLLAR AND LEASH
Before you begin your Irish Wolfhound puppy's education, he must be used to his collar and leash. Choose a collar for your puppy that is secure, but not heavy or bulky. He won't enjoy training if he's uncomfortable. A flat buckle collar is fine for every-day wear and for initial puppy training. For adult dogs, ask your breeder or an experienced sighthound trainer about training collars. Choke collars are not recommended, as Irish Wolfhounds are intelligent and

LEADER OF THE PACK
Canines are pack animals. They live according to pack rules, and every pack has only one leader. Guess what? That's you! To establish your position of authority, lay down the rules and be fair and good-natured in all your dealings with your dog. He will consider young children as his littermates, but the one who trains him, who feeds him, who grooms him, who expects him to come into line, that's his leader. And he who leads must be obeyed.

sensitive sighthounds that do not respond well to being tugged, pulled and jerked about. They require positive training methods or else you will get nowhere.

A lightweight 6-foot woven cotton or nylon training leash is preferred by most trainers because it is easy to fold up in your hand and comfortable to hold because there is a certain amount of give to it. There are lessons where the dog will start off 6 feet away from you at the end of the leash. The leash used to take the puppy outside to relieve himself is shorter because you don't want him to roam away from his area. The shorter leash will also be the one to use when you walk the puppy.

If you've been wise enough to enroll in a puppy kindergarten training class, suggestions will be made as to the best collar and leash for your young puppy. I say "wise" because your puppy will be in a class with puppies in his age range (up to five months old) of all breeds and sizes. It's the perfect way for him to learn the right way (and the wrong way) to interact with other dogs as well as their people. You cannot teach your puppy how to interpret another dog's sign language. For a first-time puppy owner, these socialization classes are invaluable. For experienced dog owners, they are a real boon to further training.

TIPS FOR TRAINING AND SAFETY

1. Whether on- or off-leash, practice only in a fenced area.
2. Remove the training collar when the training session is over.
3. Don't try to break up a dogfight.
4. "Come," "Leave it" and "Wait" are safety commands.
5. The dog belongs in a crate or behind a barrier when riding in the car.
6. Don't ignore the dog's first sign of aggression. Aggression only gets worse, so take it seriously.
7. Keep the faces of children and dogs separated.
8. Pay attention to what the dog is chewing.
9. Keep the vet's number near your phone.
10. "Okay" is a useful release command.

ATTENTION

You've been using the dog's name since the minute you collected him from the breeder, so you should be able to get his attention by saying his name—with a big smile and in an excited tone of voice. His response will be the puppy equivalent of "Here I am! What are we going to do?" Your immediate response (if you haven't guessed by now) is "Good dog." Rewarding him at the moment he pays attention to you teaches him the proper way to respond when he hears his name.

EXERCISES FOR A BASIC CANINE EDUCATION

THE SIT EXERCISE

There are several ways to teach the puppy to sit. The first one is to catch him whenever he is about to sit and, as his backside nears the floor, say "Sit, good dog!" That's positive reinforcement and, if your timing is sharp, he will learn that what he's doing at that second is connected to your saying "Sit" and that you think he's clever for doing it!

Another method is to start with the puppy on his leash in front of you. Show him a treat in the palm of your right hand.

Bring your hand up under his nose and, almost in slow motion, move your hand up and back so his nose goes up in the air and his head tilts back as he follows the treat in your hand. At that point, he will have to either sit or fall over, so as his back legs buckle under, say "Sit, good dog," and then give him the treat and lots of praise. You may have to begin with your hand lightly running up his chest, actually lifting his chin up until he sits. Some (usually older) dogs require gentle pressure on their hindquarters with the left hand, in which case the dog should be on your left side. Puppies generally do not appreciate this physical dominance.

After a few times, you should be able to show the dog a treat in the open palm of your hand, raise your hand waist-high as you say "Sit" and have him sit. You thereby will have taught him two things at the same time. Both the verbal command and the motion of the hand are signals for the sit. Your puppy is watching you almost more than he is listening to you, so what you do is just as important as what you say.

Don't save any of these drills only for training sessions. Use them as much as possible at odd times during a normal day. The dog should always sit before being given his food dish. He should sit to let you go through a doorway first, when the doorbell rings or when you stop to speak to someone on the street.

THE DOWN EXERCISE

Before beginning to teach the down command, you must consider how the dog feels about this exercise. To him, "down" is a submissive position. Being flat on the floor with you standing over him is not his idea of fun. It's up to you to let him know that, while it may not be fun, the reward of your approval is worth his effort.

Start with the puppy on your left side in a sit position. Hold the leash right above his collar in your left hand. Have an extra-special treat, such as a small piece of cooked chicken or hot dog, in your right hand. Place it at the end of the pup's nose and steadily move your hand down and

No matter the command, progress to off-leash training only in an enclosed area and after the dog has mastered the exercise on leash.

forward along the ground. Hold the leash to prevent a sudden lunge for the food. As the puppy goes into the down position, say "Down" very gently.

The difficulty with this exercise is twofold: it's both the submissive aspect and the fact that most people say the word "Down" as if they were a drill sergeant in charge of recruits! So issue the command sweetly, give him the treat and have the pup maintain the down position for several seconds. If he tries to get up immediately, place your hands on his shoulders and press down gently, giving him a very quiet "Good dog." As you progress with this lesson, increase the "down time" until he will hold it until you say "Okay" (his cue for

READY, SIT, GO!

On your marks, get set: train! Most professional trainers agree that the sit command is the place to start your dog's formal education. Sitting is a natural posture for most dogs, and they respond to the sit exercise willingly and readily. For every lesson, begin with the sit command so that you start with a successful exercise; likewise, you should practice the sit command at the end of every lesson as well because you always want to end on a high note.

Most dogs will flop into the down position on their own with no problem, but are more resistant when commanded into the down.

release). Practice this one in the house at various times throughout the day.

By increasing the length of time during which the dog must maintain the down position, you'll find many uses for it. For example, he can lie at your feet in the vet's office or anywhere that both of you have to wait, when you are on the phone, while the family is eating and so forth. If you progress to training for

---

OKAY!

This is the signal that tells your dog that he can quit whatever he was doing. Use "Okay" to end a session on a correct response to a command. (Never end on an incorrect response.) Lots of praise follows. People use "Okay" a lot and it has other uses for dogs, too. Your dog is barking. You say, "Okay! Come!" "Okay" signals him to stop the barking activity and "Come" allows him to come to you for a "Good dog."

---

competitive obedience, he'll already be all set for the exercise called the "long down."

THE STAY EXERCISE
You can teach your Irish Wolfhound to stay in the sit, down and stand positions. To teach the sit/stay, have the dog sit on your left side. Hold the leash at waist level in your left hand and let the dog know that you have a treat in your closed right hand. Step forward on your right foot as you say "Stay." Immediately turn and stand directly in front of the dog, keeping your right hand up high so he'll keep his eye on the treat hand and maintain the sit position for a count of five. Return to your original position and offer the reward.

Increase the length of the sit/stay each time until the dog can hold it for at least 30 seconds without moving. After about a week of success, move out on your right foot and take two steps before turning to face the dog. Give the "Stay" hand signal (left palm back toward the dog's head) as you leave. He gets the treat when you return and he holds the sit/stay. Increase the distance that you walk away from him before turning until you reach the length of your training leash. But don't rush it! Go back to the beginning if he moves before he should. No matter what the lesson, never be

upset by having to back up for a few days. The repetition and practice are what will make your dog reliable in these commands. It won't do any good to move on to something more difficult if the command is not mastered at the easier levels. Above all, even if you do get frustrated, never let your puppy know! Always keep a positive, upbeat attitude during training, which will transmit to your dog for positive results.

The down/stay is taught in the same way once the dog is completely reliable and steady with the down command. Again, don't rush it. With the dog in the down position on your left side, step out on your right foot as you say "Stay." Return by walking around in back of the dog and into your original position. While you are training, it's okay to murmur something like "Hold on" to encourage him to stay put.

When the dog will stay without moving when you are at a distance of 3 or 4 feet, begin to increase the length of time before you return. Be sure he holds the down on your return until you say "Okay." At that point, he gets his treat—just so he'll remember for next time that it's not over until it's over.

THE COME EXERCISE

No command is more important to the safety of your Irish Wolfhound than "Come." It is what you should say every single time you see the puppy running toward you: "Riley, come! Good dog." During playtime, run a few feet away from the puppy and turn and tell him to "Come" as he is already running to you. You can go so far as to teach your puppy two things at once if you squat down and hold out your arms. As the pup gets close to you and you're saying "Good dog," bring your right arm in about waist

Teaching the stay with a combination of the verbal command and a hand signal is an effective way to get your point across.

Always invite your Wolfhound to come to you in a happy tone of voice, greeting him with praise, petting and perhaps a tasty treat.

There is so much you can do with your well-trained Wolfhound! Dogs enjoy hiking, as it provides much-needed activity along with exciting sights and scents.

high. Now he's also learning the hand signal, an excellent device should you be on the phone when you need to get him to come to you! You'll also both be one step ahead when you enter obedience classes.

When the puppy responds to your well-timed "Come," try it with the puppy on the training leash. This time, catch him off guard, while he's sniffing a leaf or watching a bird: "Riley, come!" You may have to pause for a split second after his name to be sure you have his attention. If the puppy shows any sign of confusion, give the leash a mild jerk and take a couple of steps backward. Do not repeat the command. In this case, you should say "Good come" as he reaches you.

That's the number-one rule of training. Each command word is given just once. Anything more is nagging. You'll also notice that all commands are one word only. Even when they are actually two words, you say them as one.

Never call the dog to come to you—with or without his name— if you are angry or intend to correct him for some misbehavior. When correcting the pup, you go to him. Your dog must always connect "Come" with something pleasant and with your approval; then you can rely on his response.

Puppies, like children, have notoriously short attention spans, so don't overdo it with any of the training. Keep each lesson short. Break it up with a quick run around the yard or a ball toss, repeat the lesson and quit as soon as the pup gets it right. That way, you will always end with a "Good dog."

Life isn't perfect and neither are puppies. A time will come, often around ten months of age, when he'll become "selectively deaf" or choose to "forget" his name. He may respond by wagging his tail (and even seeming to smile at you) with a look that says "Make me!" Laugh, throw his favorite toy and skip the lesson you had planned. Pups will be pups!

THE HEEL EXERCISE
The second most important command to teach, after the come, is the heel. When you are walking

your growing puppy, you need to be in control. Besides, it looks terrible to be pulled and yanked down the street, and it's not much fun either. Your eight-to ten-week-old puppy will probably follow you everywhere, but that's his natural instinct, not your control over the situation. However, any time he does follow you, you can say "Heel" and be ahead of the game, as he will learn to associate this command with the action of following you before you even begin teaching him to heel.

There is a very precise, almost military, procedure for teaching your dog to heel. As with all other obedience training, begin with the dog on your left side. He will be in a very nice sit and you will have the training leash across your chest. Hold the loop and folded leash in your right hand. Pick up the slack leash above the

All members of the family can help train the puppy. Only adults and older children, though, should walk the adult Wolfhound.

dog in your left hand and hold it loosely at your side. Step out on your left foot as you say "Heel." If the puppy does not move, give a gentle tug or pat your left leg to get him started. If he surges ahead of you, stop and pull him back gently until he is at your side. Tell him to sit and begin again.

Walk a few steps and stop while the puppy is correctly beside you. Tell him to sit and give mild verbal praise. (More enthusiastic praise will encourage him to think the lesson is over.) Repeat the lesson, increasing the number of steps you take only as long as the dog is heeling nicely beside you. When you end the lesson, have him hold the sit, then give him the "Okay" to let him know that this is the end of the

LET'S GO!

Many people use "Let's go" instead of "Heel" when teaching their dogs to behave on lead. It sounds more like fun! When beginning to teach the heel, whatever command you use, always step off on your left foot. That's the one next to the dog, who is on your left side, in case you've forgotten. Keep a loose leash. When the dog pulls ahead, stop, bring him back and begin again. Use treats to guide him around turns.

OUR CANINE KIDS

"Everything I learned about parenting, I learned from my dog." How often adults recognize that their parenting skills are mere extensions of the education they acquired while caring for their dogs. Many owners refer to their dogs as their "kids" and treat their canine companions like real members of the family. Surveys indicate that a majority of dog owners talk to their dogs regularly, celebrate their dogs' birthdays and purchase Christmas gifts for their dogs. Another survey shows that dog owners take their dogs to the veterinarian more frequently than they visit their own physicians.

lesson. Praise him so that he knows he did a good job.

The cure for excessive pulling (a common problem) is to stop when the dog is no more than 2 or 3 feet ahead of you. Guide him back into position and begin again. With a really determined puller, try switching to a head collar. This will automatically turn the pup's head toward you so you can bring him back easily to the heel position. Give quiet, reassuring praise every time the leash goes slack and he's staying with you.

Staying and heeling can take a lot out of a dog, so provide playtime and free-running exercise to shake off the stress when the lessons are over. You don't want him to associate training with all work and no fun.

TAPERING OFF TIDBITS

Your dog has been watching you—and the hand that treats—throughout all of his lessons, and now it's time to break the treat habit. Begin by giving him treats at the end of each lesson only. Then start to give a treat after the end of only some of the lessons. At the end of every lesson, as well as during the lessons, be consistent with the praise. Your pup now doesn't know whether he'll get a treat or not, but he should keep performing well just in case! Finally, you will stop giving treat rewards entirely. Save them for something brand-new that you want to teach him. Keep up the praise and you'll always have a "good dog."

OBEDIENCE CLASSES

The advantages of an obedience class are that your dog will have to learn amid the distractions of other people and dogs and that your mistakes will be quickly corrected by the trainer. Teaching your dog along with a qualified instructor and other handlers who may have more dog experience than you is another plus of the class environment. The instructor and other handlers can help you to find the most efficient way of teaching your dog a command or exercise. It's often easier to learn by other people's mistakes than your own. You will also learn all of the requirements for competitive obedience trials, in which you can earn titles and go on to advanced jumping and retrieving exercises, which are fun for many dogs. Obedience classes build the foundation needed for many other canine activities (in which we humans are allowed to participate, too!).

TRAINING FOR OTHER ACTIVITIES

Once your dog has basic obedience under his collar and is 12 months of age, you can enter the world of agility training. Dogs think agility is pure fun, like being turned loose in an amusement park full of obstacles! If you are interested in pursuing other types of competition with your Irish Wolfhound, there are lure-coursing and racing events for sighthounds, as well as tracking, which is open to all "nosey" dogs (which would include all dogs!). For those who like to volunteer, there is the wonderful feeling of owning a therapy dog and visiting hospices, nursing homes and veterans' homes to bring smiles, comfort and companionship to those who live there.

Around the house, your Irish Wolfhound can be taught to do some simple chores. You might teach him to carry a basket of

THE BEST INVESTMENT
Obedience school is as important for you and your dog as grammar school is for your kids, and it's a lot more fun! Don't shun classes thinking that your dog might embarrass you. He might! Instructors don't expect you to know everything, but they'll teach you the correct way to teach your dog so he won't embarrass you again. He'll become a social animal as you learn with other people and dogs. Home training, while effective in teaching your dog the basic commands, excludes these socialization benefits.

household items or to fetch the morning newspaper. The kids can teach the dog all kinds of tricks, from playing hide-and-seek to balancing a biscuit on his nose. A family dog is what rounds out the family. Everything he does, including sitting at your feet and gazing lovingly at you, represents the bonus of owning a dog.

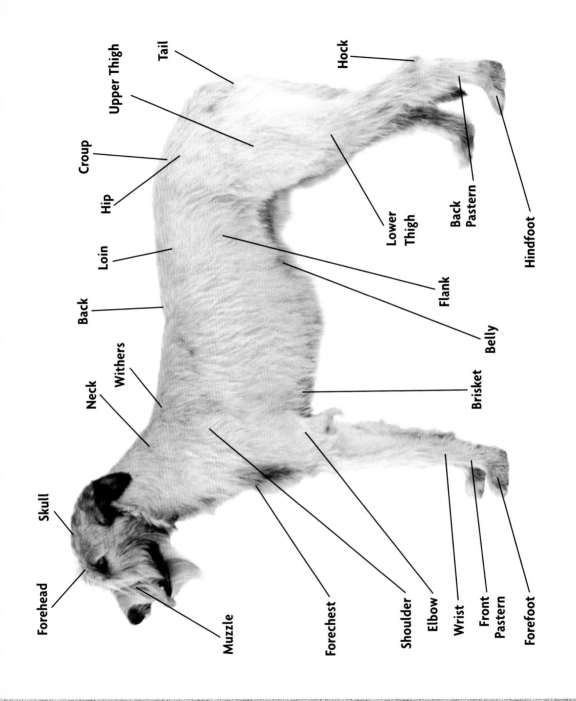

PHYSICAL STRUCTURE OF THE IRISH WOLFHOUND

BY LOWELL ACKERMAN, DVM, DACVD

HEALTHCARE FOR A LIFETIME

When you own a dog, you become his healthcare advocate over his entire lifespan, as well as being the one to shoulder the financial burden of such care. Accordingly, it is worthwhile to focus on prevention rather than treatment, as you and your pet will both be happier.

Of course, the best place to have begun your program of preventive healthcare is with the initial purchase or adoption of your dog. There is no way of guaranteeing that your new furry friend is free of medical problems, but there are some things you can do to improve your odds. You certainly should have done adequate research into the Irish Wolfhound and have selected your puppy carefully rather than buying on impulse. Health issues aside, a large number of pet abandonment and relinquishment cases arise from a mismatch between pet needs and owner expectations. This is entirely preventable with appropriate planning and finding a good breeder.

Regarding healthcare issues specifically, it is very difficult to make blanket statements about where to acquire a problem-free pet, but, again, a reputable breeder is your best bet. In an ideal situation you have the opportunity to see both parents, get references from other owners of the breeder's pups and see genetic-testing documentation for several generations of the litter's ancestors. At the very least, you must thoroughly investigate the Irish Wolfhound and the problems inherent in that breed, as well as the genetic testing available to screen for those problems. Genetic testing offers some important benefits, but testing is

One of the first things you and your new Wolfhound puppy will do together is visit the vet.

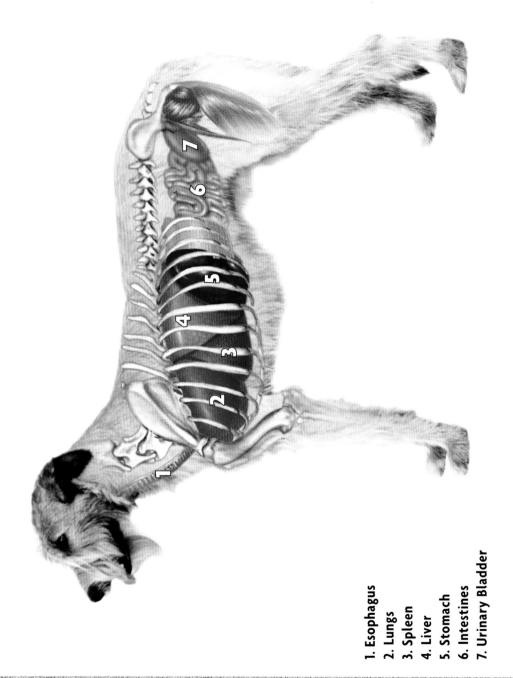

1. Esophagus
2. Lungs
3. Spleen
4. Liver
5. Stomach
6. Intestines
7. Urinary Bladder

INTERNAL ORGANS OF THE IRISH WOLFHOUND

available for only a few disorders in a relatively small number of breeds and is not available for some of the most common genetic diseases, such as hip dysplasia, cataracts, epilepsy, cardiomyopathy, etc. This area of research is indeed exciting and increasingly important, and advances will continue to be made each year. In fact, recent research has shown that there is an equivalent dog gene for 75% of known human genes, so research done in either species is likely to benefit the other.

We've also discussed that evaluating the behavioral nature of your Irish Wolfhound and that of his immediate family members is an important part of the selection process that cannot be underestimated or overemphasized. It is sometimes difficult to evaluate temperament in puppies because certain behavioral tendencies, such as some forms of aggression, may not be immediately evident. More dogs are euthanized each year for behavioral reasons than for all medical conditions combined, so it is critical to take temperament issues seriously. Start with a well-balanced, friendly companion and put the time and effort into proper socialization, and you will both be rewarded with a lifelong valued relationship.

Assuming that you have started off with a pup from

TAKING YOUR DOG'S TEMPERATURE

It is important to know how to take your dog's temperature at times when you think he may be ill. It's not the most enjoyable task, but it can be done without too much difficulty. It's easier with a helper, preferably someone with whom the dog is friendly, so that one of you can hold the dog while the other inserts the thermometer.

Before inserting the thermometer, coat the end with petroleum jelly. Insert the thermometer slowly and gently into the dog's rectum about one inch. Wait for the reading, about two minutes. Be sure to remove the thermometer carefully and clean it thoroughly after each use.

A dog's normal body temperature is between 100.5 and 102.5 degrees F. Immediate veterinary attention is required if the dog's temperature is below 99 or above 104 degrees F.

---

healthy, sound stock, you then become responsible for helping your veterinarian keep your pet healthy. Some crucial things happen before you even bring your puppy home. Parasite control typically begins at two weeks of age, and vaccinations typically begin at six to eight weeks of age. A pre-pubertal evaluation is typically scheduled for about six months of age. At this time, a dental evaluation is

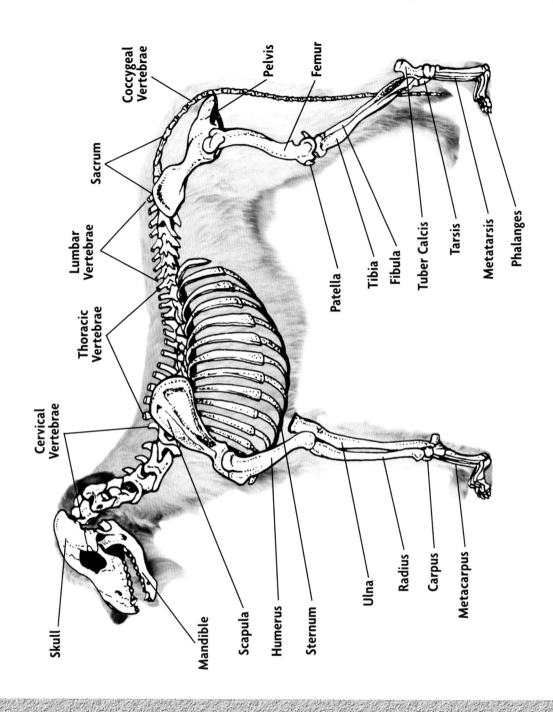

SKELETAL STRUCTURE OF THE IRISH WOLFHOUND

done (since the adult teeth are now in), heartworm prevention is started and neutering or spaying is most commonly done.

It is critical to commence regular dental care at home if you have not already done so. It may not sound very important, but most dogs have active periodontal disease by four years of age if they don't have their teeth cleaned regularly at home, not just at their veterinary exams. Dental problems lead to more than just bad "doggy breath." Gum disease can have very serious medical consequences. If you start brushing your dog's teeth and using antiseptic rinses from a young age, your dog will be accustomed to it and will not resist. The results will be healthy dentition, which your pet will need to enjoy a long, healthy life.

YOUR WOLFHOUND'S MOUTH

A veterinary dental exam is necessary if you notice one or any combination of the following in your dog:
- Broken, loose or missing teeth
- Loss of appetite (which could be due to mouth pain or illness caused by infection)
- Gum abnormalities, including redness, swelling and bleeding
- Drooling, with or without blood
- Yellowing of the teeth or gumline, indicating tartar
- Bad breath

Most dogs are considered adults at a year of age, although most larger breeds continue filling out until about two or so years old. Even individual dogs within each breed have different healthcare requirements, so work with your veterinarian to determine what will be needed and what your role should be. This doctor-client relationship is important because as vaccination guidelines change, there may not be an annual "vaccine visit" scheduled. You must make sure that you see your veterinarian at least annually, even if no vaccines are due, because this is the best opportunity to coordinate healthcare activities and to make sure that no medical issues creep by unaddressed.

A toothbrush made for the contours of a dog's mouth and specially formulated doggie toothpaste make the essential home dental care easy for owners.

When your Irish Wolfhound reaches three-quarters of his anticipated lifespan, he is considered a "senior" and likely requires some special care. In general, if you've been taking great care of your canine companion throughout his forma-tive and adult years, the transition to senior status should be a smooth one. Age is not a disease, and as long as everything is functioning as it should, there is no reason why most of late adult-hood should not be rewarding for both you and your pet. This is especially true if you have tended to the details, such as regular veterinary visits, proper dental care, excellent nutrition and management of bone and joint issues.

At this stage in your Irish Wolfhound's life, your veterinarian will want to schedule visits twice yearly, instead of once, to run some laboratory screenings, electrocardiograms and the like, and to change the diet to something more digestible. Catching problems early is the best way to manage them effectively. Treating the early stages of heart disease is so much easier than trying to intervene when there is more significant damage to the heart muscle. Similarly, managing the beginning of kidney problems is fairly routine if there is no significant kidney damage. Other problems, like cognitive dysfunction (similar to senility and Alzheimer's disease), cancer, diabetes and arthritis, are more common in older dogs, but all can be treated to help the dog live as many happy, comfortable years as possible. Just as in people, medical management for

PROBLEM: AND THAT STARTS WITH "P"

Urinary tract problems more commonly affect female dogs, especially those who have been spayed. The first sign that a urinary tract problem exists usually is a strong odor from the urine or an unusual color. Blood in the urine, known as hematuria, is another sign of an infection, related to cystitis, a bladder infection, bladder cancer or a blood-clotting disorder. Urinary tract problems can also be signaled by the dog's straining while urinating, experiencing pain during urination and genital discharge as well as excessive water intake and urination.

Excessive drinking, in and of itself, does not indicate a urinary tract problem. A dog who is drinking more than normal may have a kidney or liver problem, a hormonal disorder or diabetes mellitus. Behaviorists report a disorder known as psychogenic polydipsia, which manifests itself in excessive drinking and urination. If you notice your dog drinking much more than normal, take him to the vet.

pets is more effective (and less expensive) when you catch things early.

SELECTING A VETERINARIAN

There is probably no more important decision that you will make regarding your pet's healthcare than the selection of his doctor. Your pet's veterinarian will be a pediatrician, family-practice physician and gerontologist, depending on the dog's life stage, and will be the individual who makes recommendations regarding issues such as when specialists need to be consulted, when diagnostic testing and/or therapeutic intervention is needed and when you will need to seek outside emergency and critical-care services. Your vet will act as your advocate and liaison throughout these processes.

Everyone has his own idea about what to look for in a vet, an individual who will play a big role in his dog's (and, of course, his own) life for many years to come. For some, it is the compassionate caregiver with whom they hope to develop a professional relationship to span the lifetime of their dogs and even their future pets. For others, they are seeking a clinician with keen diagnostic and therapeutic insight who can deliver state-of-the-art healthcare. Still others need a veterinary facility that is open evenings and weekends, is

YOUR DOG NEEDS TO VISIT THE VET IF:

- He has ingested a toxin such as antifreeze or a toxic plant; in these cases, administer first aid and call the vet right away;
- His teeth are discolored, loose or missing or he has sores or other signs of infection or abnormality in the mouth;
- He has been vomiting, has had diarrhea or has been constipated for over 24 hours; call immediately if you notice blood;
- He has refused food for over 24 hours;
- His eating habits, water intake or toilet habits have noticeably changed; if you have noticed weight gain or weight loss;
- He shows symptoms of bloat, which requires *immediate* attention;
- He is salivating excessively;
- He has a lump in his throat;
- He has a lump or bumps anywhere on the body;
- He is very lethargic;
- He appears to be in pain or otherwise has trouble; chewing or swallowing
- His skin loses elasticity.

Of course, there will be other instances in which a visit to the vet is necessary; these are just some of the signs that could be indicative of serious problems that need to be caught as early as possible.

The Eyes Have It!

Eye disease is more prevalent among dogs than most people think, ranging from slight infections that are easily treated to serious complications that can lead to permanent sight loss. Eye diseases need veterinary attention in their early stages to prevent irreparable damage. This list provides descriptions of some common eye diseases:

Cataracts: Symptoms are white or gray discoloration of the eye lens and pupil, which causes fuzzy or completely obscured vision. Surgical treatment is required to remove the damaged lens and replace it with an artificial one.

Conjunctivitis: An inflammation of the mucus membrane that lines the eye socket, leaving the eyes red and puffy with excessive discharge. This condition is easily treated with antibiotics.

Corneal damage: The cornea is the transparent covering of the iris and pupil. Injuries are difficult to detect, but manifest themselves in surface abnormality, redness, pain and discharge. Most infections of the cornea are treated with antibiotics and require immediate medical attention.

Dry eye: This condition is caused by deficient production of tears that lubricate and protect the eye surface. A telltale sign is yellow-green discharge. Left undiagnosed, your dog will experience considerable pain, infections and possibly blindness. Dry eye is commonly treated with antibiotics, although more advanced cases may require surgery.

Glaucoma: This is caused by excessive fluid pressure in the eye. Symptoms are red eyes, gray or blue discoloration, pain, enlarged eyeballs and loss of vision. Antibiotics sometimes help, but surgery may be needed.

in close proximity or provides mobile veterinary services to accommodate their schedules; these people may not much mind that their dogs might see different veterinarians on each visit. Just as we have different reasons for selecting our own healthcare professionals (e.g., covered by insurance plan, expert in field, convenient location, etc.), we should not expect that there is a one-size-fits-all recommendation for selecting a veterinarian and veterinary practice. The best advice is to be honest in your assessment of what you expect

from a veterinary practice and to conscientiously research the options in your area. You will quickly appreciate that not all veterinary practices are the same, and you will be happiest with one that truly meets your needs.

There is another point to be considered in the selection of veterinary services. Not that long ago, a single veterinarian would attempt to manage all medical and surgical issues as they arose. That was often problematic because veterinarians are trained in many species and many diseases, and it was just impossible for general veterinary practitioners to be experts in every species, every breed, every field and every ailment. However, just as in the human healthcare fields, specialization has allowed general practitioners to concentrate on primary healthcare delivery, especially wellness and the prevention of infectious diseases, and to utilize a network of specialists to assist in the management of conditions that require specific expertise and experience. Thus there are now many types of veterinary specialists, including dermatologists, cardiologists, ophthalmologists, surgeons, internists, oncologists, neurologists, behaviorists, criticalists and others to help primary-care veterinarians deal with complicated medical challenges. In most cases, specialists see cases referred by primary-care veterinarians, make diagnoses and set up management plans. From there, the animals' ongoing care is returned to their primary-care veterinarians. This important team approach to your pet's medical-care needs has provided opportunities for advanced care and an unparalleled level of quality to be delivered.

With all of the opportunities for your Irish Wolfhound to receive high-quality veterinary medical care, there is another topic that needs to be addressed at the same time—cost. It's been said that you can have excellent healthcare or inexpensive healthcare, but never both; this is as true in veterinary medicine as it is in human medicine. While veterinary costs are a fraction of what the same services cost in the human healthcare arena, it is still difficult to deal with unanticipated medical costs, especially since they can easily creep into hundreds or even thousands of dollars if specialists or emergency services become involved. However, there are ways of managing these risks. The easiest is to buy pet health insurance and realize that its foremost purpose is not to cover routine healthcare visits but rather to serve as an umbrella for those rainy days when your pet needs medical care and you don't want to worry about whether or not you can afford that care.

Pet insurance policies are very cost-effective (and very inexpensive by human health-insurance standards), but make sure that you buy the policy long before you intend to use it (preferably starting in puppyhood, because coverage will exclude pre-existing conditions) and that you are actually buying an indemnity insurance plan from an insurance company that is regulated by your state or province. Many insurance policy look-alikes are actually discount clubs that are redeemable only at

Common Infectious Diseases

Let's discuss some of the diseases that create the need for vaccination in the first place. Following are the major canine infectious diseases and a simple explanation of each.

Rabies: A devastating viral disease that can be fatal in dogs and people. In fact, vaccination of dogs and cats is an important public-health measure to create a resistant animal buffer population to protect people from contracting the disease. Vaccination schedules are determined on a government level and are not optional for pet owners; rabies vaccination is required by law in all 50 states.

Parvovirus: A severe, potentially life-threatening disease that is easily transmitted between dogs. There are four strains of the virus, but it is believed that there is significant "cross-protection" between strains that may be included in individual vaccines.

Distemper: A potentially severe and life-threatening disease with a relatively high risk of exposure, especially in certain regions. In very high-risk distemper environments, young pups may be vaccinated with human measles vaccine, a related virus that offers cross-protection when administered at four to ten weeks of age.

Hepatitis: Caused by canine adenovirus type 1 (CAV-1), but since vaccination with the causative virus has a higher rate of adverse effects, cross-protection is derived from the use of adenovirus type 2 (CAV-2), a cause of respiratory disease and one of the potential causes of canine cough. Vaccination with CAV-2 provides long-term immunity against hepatitis, but relatively less protection against respiratory infection.

Canine cough: Also called tracheobronchitis, actually a fairly complicated result of viral and bacterial offenders; therefore, even with vaccination, protection is incomplete. Wherever dogs congregate, canine cough will likely be spread among them. Intranasal vaccination with *Bordetella* and parainfluenza is the best safeguard, but the duration of immunity does not appear to be very long, typically a year at most. These are non-core vaccines, but vaccination is sometimes mandated by boarding kennels, obedience classes, dog shows and other places where dogs congregate to try to minimize spread of infection.

Leptospirosis: A potentially fatal disease that is more common in some geographic regions. It is capable of being spread to humans. The disease varies with the individual "serovar," or strain, of *Leptospira* involved. Since there does not appear to be much cross-protection between serovars, protection is only as good as the likelihood that the serovar in the vaccine is the same as the one in the pet's local environment. Problems with *Leptospira* vaccines are that protection does not last very long, side effects are not uncommon and a large percentage of dogs (perhaps 30%) may not respond to vaccination.

Borrelia burgdorferi: The cause of Lyme disease, the risk of which varies with the geographic area in which the pet lives and travels. Lyme disease is spread by deer ticks in the eastern US and western black-legged ticks in the western part of the country, and the risk of exposure is high in some regions. Lameness, fever and inappetence are most commonly seen in affected dogs. The extent of protection from the vaccine has not been conclusively demonstrated.

Coronavirus: This disease has a high risk of exposure, especially in areas where dogs congregate, but it typically causes only mild to moderate digestive upset (diarrhea, vomiting, etc.). Vaccines are available, but the duration of protection is believed to be relatively short and the effectiveness of the vaccine in preventing infection is considered low.

There are many other vaccinations available, including those for *Giardia* and canine adenovirus-1. While there may be some specific indications for their use, and local risk factors to be considered, they are not widely recommended for most dogs.

specific locations and for specific services. An indemnity plan covers your pet at almost all veterinary, specialty and emergency practices and is an excellent way to manage your pet's ongoing healthcare needs.

VACCINATIONS AND INFECTIOUS DISEASES

There has never been an easier time to prevent a variety of infectious diseases in your dog, but the advances we've made in veterinary medicine come with a price—choice. Now while it may seem that choice regarding your pet's vaccinations is a good thing, it also has never been more difficult for the pet owner (or the veterinarian) to make an informed decision about the best way to protect pets through vaccination.

Years ago, it was just accepted that puppies got a starter series of vaccinations and then annual "boosters" throughout their lives to keep them protected. As more and more vaccines became available, consumers wanted the convenience of having all of that protection in a single injection. The result was "multivalent" vaccines that crammed a lot of protection into a single syringe. The manufacturers' recommendations were to give the vaccines annually, and this was a simple enough protocol to follow. However, as veterinary medicine has become more sophisticated and we have started looking more at healthcare quandaries rather than convenience, it became necessary to reevaluate the situation and deal with some tough questions. It is important to realize that whether or not to use a particular vaccine depends on the risk of contracting the disease against which it protects, the severity of the disease if it is contracted, the duration of immunity provided by the vaccine, the safety of the product and the needs of the individual animal. In a very general sense, rabies, distemper, hepatitis and parvovirus are considered core vaccine needs, while parainfluenza, *Bordetella bronchiseptica*, leptospirosis, coronavirus and borreliosis (Lyme disease) are considered non-core needs and best reserved for animals that demonstrate reasonable risk of contracting the diseases.

NEUTERING/SPAYING

Sterilization procedures (neutering for males/spaying for females) are meant to accomplish several purposes. While the underlying premise is to address the risk of pet overpopulation, there are also some medical and behavioral benefits to the surgeries as well. For females, spaying prior to the first estrus (heat cycle) leads to a marked reduction in the risk of mammary cancer. There also will be no manifestations of "heat" to attract male dogs and no bleeding in the house. For males, there is prevention of testicular cancer and a reduction in the risk of prostate problems. In both sexes there may be some limited reduction in aggressive behaviors toward other dogs, and some diminishing of urine marking, roaming and mounting.

While neutering and spaying do indeed prevent animals from contributing to pet overpopulation, even no-cost and low-cost neutering options have not eliminated the problem. Perhaps one of the main reasons for this is that individuals that intentionally breed their dogs and those that allow their animals to run at large are the main causes of unwanted offspring. Also, animals in shel-

BLOAT-PREVENTION TIPS

As varied as the causes of bloat are the tips for prevention, but some common preventive methods follow:

▶ Feed two or three small meals daily rather than one large one;

▶ Do not feed water before, after or with meals, but allow access to water at all other times;

▶ Never permit rapid eating or gulping of water;

▶ No exercise for the dog at least two hours before and (especially) after meals;

▶ Feed high-quality food with adequate protein, adequate fiber content and not too much fat and carbohydrate;

▶ Explore herbal additives, enzymes or gas-reduction products (only under a vet's advice) to encourage a "friendly" environment in the dog's digestive system;

▶ Avoid foods and ingredients known to produce gas;

▶ Avoid stressful situations for the dog, especially at mealtimes;

▶ Make dietary changes gradually, over a period of a few weeks;

▶ Do not feed dry food only;

▶ Although the role of genetics as a causative of bloat is not known, many breeders do not breed from previously affected dogs;

▶ Sometimes owners are advised to have gastroplexy (stomach stapling) performed on their dogs as a preventive measure.

Of utmost importance is that you know your dog! Pay attention to his behavior and any changes that could be symptomatic of bloat. Your dog's life depends on it!

Don't Eat the Daisies!

Many plants and flowers are beautiful to look at, but can be highly toxic if ingested by your dog. Reactions range from abdominal pain and vomiting to convulsions and death. If the following plants are in your home, remove them. If they are outside your house or in your garden, avoid accidents by removing them or making sure your dog is never left unsupervised in those locations.

Azalea
Belladonna
Bird of paradise
Bulbs
Calla lily
Cardinal flower
Castor bean
Chinaberry tree
Daphne

Dumb cane
Dutchman's breeches
Elephant's ear
Hydrangea
Jack-in-the-pulpit
Jasmine
Jimsonweed
Larkspur
Laurel
Lily of the valley

Mescal bean
Mushrooms
Nightshade
Philodendron
Poinsettia
Prunus species
Tobacco
Yellow jasmine
Yews, *Taxus* species

ters are often there because they were abandoned or relinquished, not because they came from unplanned matings. Neutering/spaying is important, but it should be considered in the context of the real causes of animals' ending up in shelters and eventually being euthanized.

One of the important considerations regarding neutering is that it is a surgical procedure. This sometimes gets lost in discussions of low-cost procedures and commoditization of the process. In females, spaying is specifically referred to as an ovariohysterectomy. In this procedure, a midline incision is made in the abdomen and the entire uterus and both ovaries are surgically removed. While this is a major invasive surgical procedure, it usually has few complications because it is typically performed on healthy young animals. However, it is major surgery, as any woman who has had a hysterectomy will attest.

In males, neutering has traditionally referred to castration, which involves the surgical removal of both testicles. While still a significant piece of surgery, there is not the abdominal exposure that is required in the female surgery. In addition, there is now a chemical sterilization

Dogs of any breed can suffer from allergies. These two furry companions are susceptible to many of the same allergens, not to mention parasites that may lurk in the grass. Keep an eye on your dog's condition with thorough skin and coat checks after time spent outdoors.

FOOD ALLERGY

Severe itching, leading to bald patches and open sores on the feet, face, ears, armpits and groin, could be caused by a food allergy. Studies indicate that up to 10% of dogs suffer from food allergies. Dogs who suffer from chronic ear problems may actually have a food allergy. Unfortunately, there are no tests available to determine whether your dog definitely suffers from a food allergy. The dog will be miserable and you will be frustrated and stressed.

Take the problem into your own hands and kitchen. Select a type of meat that your dog is not getting from his existing diet, perhaps white fish, lamb or venison, and prepare a home-cooked food. The food should consist of two parts carbohydrate (rice, pasta or potatoes) and one part protein (the chosen meat). It's better not to start with soy as the protein source unless all of the meats cause a reaction.

Monitor your dog's intake carefully. He must eat only your prepared meal without any extras. All family members (and visiting friends) must be informed of the plan. After four or five weeks on the new diet, you will reintroduce a portion of his original diet to determine whether this food is the cause of the allergic reactions. Once the dog reacts to the change in diet, resume the new diet. Make dietary modifications every two weeks and keep careful records of any reactions the dog has to the diet.

option, in which a solution is injected into each testicle, leading to atrophy of the sperm-producing cells. This can typically be done under sedation rather than full anesthesia. This is a relatively new approach, and there are no long-term clinical studies yet available.

Neutering/spaying is typically done around six months of age at

will definitely not produce any pups. Otherwise, these organizations need to rely on owners to comply with their wishes to have the animals "altered" at a later date, something that does not always happen.

There are some exciting immunocontraceptive "vaccines" currently under development, and there may be a time when contraception in pets will not require surgical procedures. We anxiously await these developments.

most veterinary hospitals, although techniques have been pioneered to perform the procedures in animals as young as eight weeks of age. In general, the surgeries on the very young animals are done for the specific reason of sterilizing them before they go to their new homes. This is done in some shelter hospitals for assurance that the animals

THREADWORMS

Though less common than ascarids, hookworms and other nematodes, threadworms concern dog owners in the southwestern US and Gulf Coast area where the climate is hot and humid. Living in the small intestine of the dog, this worm measures a mere 2 millimeters and is round in shape. Like that of the whipworm, the threadworm's life cycle is very complex, and the eggs and larvae are passed through the feces. The cause of a deadly disease in humans, worms of the genus *Strongyloides* readily infect people; the handling of feces is the most common means of transmission. Threadworms are most often seen in young puppies; bloody diarrhea and pneumonia are symptoms. Sick puppies must be isolated and treated immediately; vets recommend a follow-up treatment one month later.

S. E. M. by Dr. Dennis Kunkel, University of Hawaii

A scanning electron micrograph of a dog flea, *Ctenocephalides canis*, on dog hair.

EXTERNAL PARASITES

FLEAS

Fleas have been around for millions of years and, while we have better tools now for controlling them than at any time in the past, there still is little chance that they will end up on an endangered species list. Actually, they are very well adapted to living on our pets, and they continue to adapt as we make advances.

The female flea can consume 15 times her weight in blood during active reproduction and can lay as many as 40 eggs a day. These eggs are very resistant to the effects of insecticides. They hatch into larvae, which then mature and spin cocoons. The immature fleas reside in this pupal stage until the time is right for feeding. This pupal stage is also very resistant to the effects of insecticides, and pupae can last in the environment without feeding for many months. Newly emergent fleas are attracted to animals by the warmth of the animals' bodies, movement and exhaled carbon dioxide. However, when they first emerge from their cocoons, they orient towards light; thus when an animal passes between a flea and the light source, casting a shadow, the flea pounces and starts to feed. If the animal turns out to be a dog or cat, the reproductive cycle continues. If the flea lands on another type of animal, including a person, the flea will bite but will then look for a more appropriate host. An emerging adult flea can survive without feeding for up to 12 months but, once it tastes blood, it can survive off its host for only 3 to 4 days.

It was once thought that fleas spend most of their lives in the environment, but we now know that fleas won't willingly jump off a dog unless leaping to another dog or when physically removed by brushing, bathing or other manipulation. Flea eggs, on the other hand, are shiny and smooth, and they roll off the animal and into the environment. The eggs, larvae and pupae then exist in the environment, but once the adult finds a susceptible animal, it's home sweet home until the flea is forced to seek refuge elsewhere.

Since adult fleas live on the animal and immature forms survive in the environment, a successful treatment plan must address all stages of the flea life cycle. There are now several safe and effective flea-control products that can be applied on a monthly

FLEA PREVENTION FOR YOUR DOG

- Discuss with your veterinarian the safest product to protect your dog, likely in the form of a monthly tablet or a liquid preparation placed on the back of the dog's neck.
- For dogs suffering from flea-bite dermatitis, a shampoo or topical insecticide treatment is required.
- Your lawn and property should be sprayed with an insecticide designed to kill fleas and ticks that lurk outdoors.
- Using a flea comb, check the dog's coat regularly for any signs of parasites.
- Practice good housekeeping. Vacuum floors, carpets and furniture regularly, especially in the areas that the dog frequents, and wash the dog's bedding weekly.
- Follow up house-cleaning with carpet shampoos and sprays to rid the house of fleas at all stages of development. Insect growth regulators are the safest option.

basis. These include fipronil, imidacloprid, selamectin and permethrin (found in several formulations). Most of these products have significant flea-killing rates within 24 hours. However, none of them will control the immature forms in the environment. To accomplish this, there are a variety of insect growth regulators that can be sprayed into

THE FLEA'S LIFE CYCLE

What came first, the flea or the egg? This age-old mystery is more difficult to comprehend than the actual cycle of the flea. Fleas usually live only about four months. A female can lay 2,000 eggs in her lifetime.

Egg

After ten days of rolling around your carpet or under your furniture, the eggs hatch into larvae, which feed on various and sundry debris.

Larva

In days or months, depending on the climate, the larvae spin cocoons and develop into the pupal or nymph stage, which quickly develop into fleas.

Pupa

These immature fleas must locate a host within 10 to 14 days or they will die. Only about 1% of the flea population exist as adult fleas, while the other 99% exist as eggs, larvae or pupae.

Adult

Photo by Carolina Biological Supply Co.

KILL FLEAS THE NATURAL WAY

If you choose not to go the route of conventional medication, there are some natural ways to ward off fleas:

- Dust your dog with a natural flea powder, composed of such herbal goodies as rosemary, wormwood, pennyroyal, citronella, rue, tobacco powder and eucalyptus.
- Apply diatomaceous earth, the fossilized remains of single-cell algae, to your carpets, furniture and pet's bedding. Even though it's not good for dogs, it's even worse for fleas, which will dry up swiftly and die.
- Brush your dog frequently, give him adequate exercise and let him fast occasionally. All of these activities strengthen the dog's system and make him more resistant to disease and parasites.
- Bathe your dog with a capful of pennyroyal or eucalyptus oil.
- Feed a natural diet, free of additives and preservatives. Add some fresh garlic and brewer's yeast to the dog's morning portion, as these items have flea-repelling properties.

the environment (e.g., pyriprox-yfen, methoprene, fenoxycarb) as well as insect development inhibitors such as lufenuron that can be administered. These compounds have no effect on adult fleas, but they stop immature forms from developing into adults. In years gone by, we relied heavily on toxic insecticides (such as organophosphates, organochlorines and carbamates) to manage the flea problem, but today's options are not only much safer to use on our pets but also safer for the environment.

TICKS

Ticks are members of the spider class (arachnids) and are blood-sucking parasites capable of transmitting a variety of diseases, including Lyme disease, ehrlichiosis, babesiosis and Rocky Mountain spotted fever. It's easy to see ticks on your own skin, but it is more of a challenge when your furry companion is affected. Whenever you happen to be planning a stroll in a tick-infested area (especially forests, grassy or wooded areas or parks) be prepared to do a thorough inspection of your dog afterward to search for ticks. Ticks can be tricky, so make sure you spend time looking in the ears, between the toes and everywhere else where a tick might hide. Ticks need to be attached for 24–72 hours before they transmit most of the diseases that they carry, so you do have a window of opportunity for some preventive intervention.

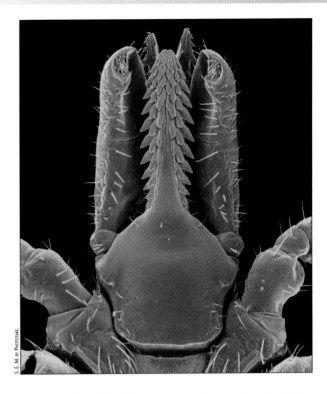

S. E. M. BY PHOTOTAKE.

A TICKING BOMB

There is nothing good about a tick's harpooning his nose into your dog's skin. Among the diseases caused by ticks are Rocky Mountain spotted fever, canine ehrlichiosis, canine babesiosis, canine hepatozoonosis and Lyme disease. If a dog is allergic to the saliva of a female wood tick, he can develop tick paralysis.

Female ticks live to eat and breed. They can lay between 4,000 and 5,000 eggs and they die soon after. Males, on the other hand, live only to mate with the females and continue the process as long as they are able. Most ticks live on multiple hosts before parasitizing dogs. The immature forms typically reside on grass and shrubs, waiting for susceptible animals to walk by. The larvae and nymph stages typically feed on wildlife.

If only a few ticks are present on a dog, they can be plucked out, but it is important to remove the entire head and mouthparts,

A scanning electron micrograph of the head of a female deer tick, *Ixodes dammini*, a parasitic tick that carries Lyme disease.

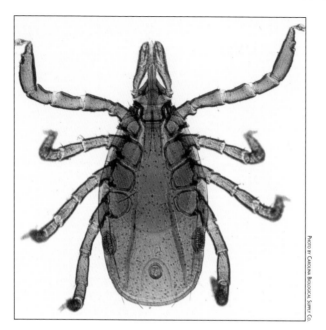

PHOTO BY CAROLINA BIOLOGICAL SUPPLY CO.

Deer tick,
Ixodes dammini.

which may be deeply embedded in the skin. This is best accomplished with forceps designed especially for this purpose; fingers can be used but should be protected with rubber gloves, plastic wrap or at least a paper towel. The tick should be grasped as closely as possible to the animal's skin and should be pulled upward with steady, even pressure. Do not squeeze, crush or puncture the body of the tick or you risk exposure to any disease carried by that tick. Once the ticks have been removed, the sites of attachment should be disinfected. Your hands should then be washed with soap and water to further minimize risk of contagion. The tick should be disposed

of in a container of alcohol or household bleach.

Some of the newer flea products, specifically those with fipronil, selamectin and permethrin, have effect against some, but not all, species of tick. Flea collars containing appropriate pesticides (e.g., propoxur, chlorfenvinphos) can aid in tick control. In most areas, such collars should be placed on animals in March, at the beginning of the tick season, and changed regularly. Leaving the collar on when the pesticide level is waning invites the development of resistance. Amitraz collars are also good for tick control, and the active ingredient does not interfere with other flea-control products. The ingredient helps prevent the attachment of ticks to the skin and will cause those ticks already on the skin to detach themselves.

TICK CONTROL

Removal of underbrush and leaf litter and the thinning of trees in areas where tick control is desired are recommended. These actions remove the cover and food sources for small animals that serve as hosts for ticks. With continued mowing of grasses in these areas, the probability of ticks' surviving is further reduced. A variety of insecticide ingredients (e.g., resmethrin, carbaryl, permethrin, chlorpyrifos, dioxathion and allethrin) are registered for tick control around the home.

MITES

Mites are tiny arachnid parasites that parasitize the skin of dogs. Skin diseases caused by mites are referred to as "mange," and there are many different forms seen in dogs. These forms are very different from one another, each one warranting an individual description.

Sarcoptic mange, or scabies, is one of the itchiest conditions that affects dogs. The microscopic *Sarcoptes* mites burrow into the superficial layers of the skin and can drive dogs crazy with itchiness. They are also communicable to people, although they can't complete their reproductive cycle on people. In addition to being tiny, the mites also are often difficult to find when trying to make a diagnosis. Skin scrapings from multiple areas are examined microscopically but, even then, sometimes the mites cannot be found.

Fortunately, scabies is relatively easy to treat, and there are a variety of products that will successfully kill the mites. Since the mites can't live in the environment for very long without feeding, a complete cure is usually possible within four to eight weeks.

Cheyletiellosis is caused by a relatively large mite, which sometimes can be seen even without a microscope. Often referred to as "walking dandruff," this also causes itching, but not usually as profound as with scabies. While *Cheyletiella* mites can survive somewhat longer

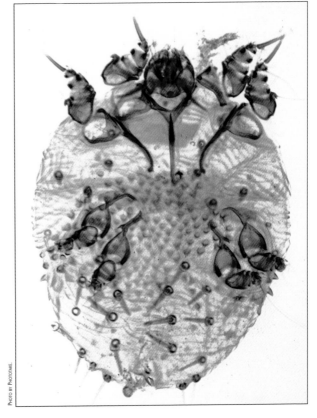

PHOTO BY PHOTOTAKE.

Sarcoptes scabiei, commonly known as the "itch mite."

in the environment than scabies mites, they too are relatively easy to treat, being responsive to not only the medications used to treat scabies but also often to flea-control products.

Otodectes cynotis is the canine ear mite and is one of the more common causes of mange, especially in young dogs in shelters or pet stores. That's because the mites are typically present in large numbers and are quickly spread to nearby animals. The mites rarely do much harm but

Micrograph of a dog louse, *Heterodoxus spiniger*. Female lice attach their eggs to the hairs of the dog. As the eggs hatch, the larval lice bite and feed on the blood. Lice can also feed on dead skin and hair. This feeding activity can cause hair loss and skin problems.

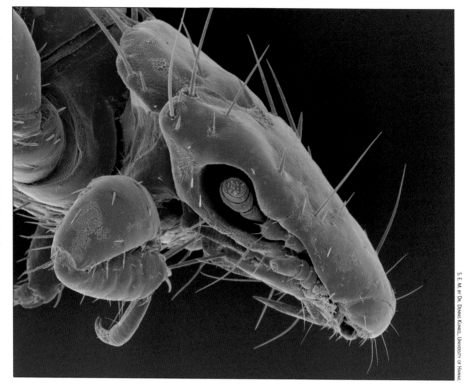

S. E. M. BY DR. DENNIS KUNKEL, UNIVERSITY OF HAWAII.

can be difficult to eradicate if the treatment regimen is not comprehensive. While many try to treat the condition with ear drops only, this is the most common cause of treatment failure. Ear drops cause the mites to simply move out of the ears and as far away as possible (usually to the base of the tail) until the insecticide levels in the ears drop to an acceptable level—then it's back to business as usual! The successful treatment of ear mites requires treating all animals in the household with a systemic insecticide, such as selamectin, or a combination of miticidal ear drops combined with whole-body flea-control preparations.

Demodicosis, sometimes referred to as red mange, can be one of the most difficult forms of mange to treat. Part of the problem has to do with the fact that the mites live in the hair follicles and they are relatively well shielded from topical and systemic products. The main issue, however, is that demodectic mange typically results only when there is some underlying process interfering with the dog's immune system.

Since *Demodex* mites are normal residents of the skin of

mammals, including humans, there is usually a mite population explosion only when the immune system fails to keep the number of mites in check. In young animals, the immune deficit may be transient or may reflect an actual inherited immune problem. In older animals, demodicosis is usually seen only when there is another disease hampering the immune system, such as diabetes, cancer, thyroid problems or the use of immune-suppressing drugs. Accordingly, treatment involves not only trying to kill the mange mites but also discerning what is interfering with immune function and correcting it if possible.

Chiggers represent several different species of mite that don't parasitize dogs specifically, but do latch on to passersby and can cause irritation. The problem is most prevalent in wooded areas in the late summer and fall. Treatment is not difficult, as the mites do not complete their life cycle on dogs and are susceptible to a variety of miticidal products.

MOSQUITOES

Mosquitoes have long been known to transmit a variety of diseases to people, as well as just being biting pests during warm weather. They also pose a real risk to pets. Not only do they carry deadly heartworms but recently there also has been much concern over their involvement with West Nile virus. While we can avoid heartworm with the use of preventive medications, there are no such preventives for West Nile virus. The only method of prevention in endemic areas is active mosquito control. Fortunately, most dogs that have been exposed to the virus only developed flu-like symptoms and, to date, there have not been the large number of reported deaths in canines as seen in some other species.

Illustration of *Demodex folliculoram.*

ILLUSTRATION BY PHOTOTAKE

MOSQUITO REPELLENT

Low concentrations of DEET (less than 10%), found in many human mosquito repellents, have been safely used in dogs but, in these concentrations, probably give only about two hours of protection. DEET may be safe in these small concentrations, but since it is not licensed for use on dogs, there is no research proving its safety for dogs. Products containing permethrin give the longest-lasting protection, perhaps two to four weeks. As DEET is not licensed for use on dogs, and both DEET and permethrin can be quite toxic to cats, appropriate care should be exercised. Other products, such as those containing oil of citronella, also have some mosquito-repellent activity, but typically have a relatively short duration of action.

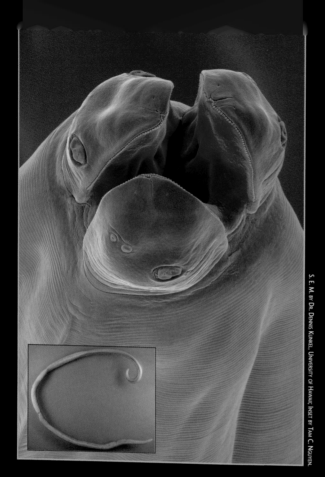

ASCARID DANGERS
The most commonly encountered worms in dogs are roundworms known as ascarids. *Toxascaris leonine* and *Toxocara canis* are the two species that infect dogs. Subsisting in the dog's stomach and intestines, adult round-worms can grow to 7 inches in length and adult females can lay in excess of 200,000 eggs in a single day.

In humans, visceral larval migrans affects people who have ingested eggs of *Toxocara canis*, which frequently contaminates children's sandboxes, beaches and park grounds. The round-worms reside in the human's stomach and intestines, as they would in a dog's, but do not mature. Instead, they find their way to the liver, lungs and skin, or even to the heart or kidneys in severe cases. Deworming puppies is critical in preventing the infection in humans, and young children should never handle nursing pups who have not been dewormed.

The ascarid roundworm *Toxocara canis,* showing the mouth with three lips. INSET: Photomicrograph of the roundworm *Ascaris lumbricoides.*

INTERNAL PARASITES: WORMS

ASCARIDS

Ascarids are intestinal round-worms that rarely cause severe disease in dogs. Nonetheless, they are of major public health signifi-cance because they can be trans-ferred to people. Sadly, it is chil-dren who are most commonly affected by the parasite, probably from inadvertently ingesting ascarid-contaminated soil. In fact, many yards and children's sand-boxes contain appreciable numbers of ascarid eggs. So, while ascarids don't bite dogs or latch onto their intestines to suck blood, they do cause some nasty medical conditions in children and are best eradicated from our furry friends. Because pups can start passing ascarid eggs by three weeks of age, most parasite-control programs begin at two weeks of age and are repeated every two weeks until pups are eight weeks old. It is important to

HOOKED ON ANCYLOSTOMA

Adult dogs can become infected by the bloodsucking nematodes we commonly call hookworms via ingesting larvae from the ground or via the larvae penetrating the dog's skin. It is not uncommon for infected dogs to show no symptoms of hookworm infestation. Sometimes symptoms occur within ten days of exposure. These symptoms can include bloody diarrhea, anemia, loss of weight and general weakness. Dogs pass the hookworm eggs in their stools, which serves as the vet's method of identifying the infestation. The hookworm larvae can encyst themselves in the dog's tissues and be released when the dog is experiencing stress.

Caused by an *Ancylostoma* species whose common host is the dog, cutaneous larval migrans affects humans, causing itching and lumps and streaks beneath the surface of the skin.

S. E. M. BY DR. DENNIS KUNKEL, UNIVERSITY OF HAWAII.

realize that bitches can pass ascarids to their pups even if they test negative prior to whelping. Accordingly, bitches are best treated at the same time as the pups.

HOOKWORMS

Unlike ascarids, hookworms do latch onto a dog's intestinal tract and can cause significant loss of blood and protein. Similar to ascarids, hookworms can be transmitted to humans, where they cause a condition known as cutaneous larval migrans. Dogs can become infected either by consuming the infective larvae or by the larvae's penetrating the skin directly. People most often get infected when they are lying on the ground (such as on a beach) and the larvae penetrate the skin. Yes, the larvae can penetrate through a beach blanket. Hookworms are typically susceptible to the same medications used to treat ascarids.

The hookworm *Ancylostoma caninum* infests the intestines of dogs. INSET: Note the row of hooks at the posterior end, used to anchor the worm to the intestinal wall.

WHIPWORMS

Whipworms latch onto the lower aspects of the dog's colon and can cause cramping and diarrhea. Eggs do not start to appear in the dog's feces until about three months after the dog was infected. This worm has a peculiar life cycle, which makes it more difficult to control than ascarids or hookworms. The good thing is that whipworms rarely are transferred to people.

Some of the medications used to treat ascarids and hookworms are also effective against whipworms, but, in general, a separate treatment protocol is needed. Since most of the medications are effective against the adults but not the eggs or larvae, treatment is typically repeated in three weeks, and then often in three

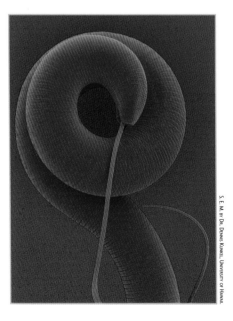

Adult whipworm, *Trichuris* sp., an intestinal parasite.

S. E. M. BY DR. DENNIS KUNKEL, UNIVERSITY OF HAWAII.

WORM-CONTROL GUIDELINES

- Practice sanitary habits with your dog and home.
- Clean up after your dog and don't let him sniff or eat other dogs' droppings.
- Control insects and fleas in the dog's environment. Fleas, lice, cockroaches, beetles, mice and rats can act as hosts for various worms.
- Prevent dogs from eating uncooked meat, raw poultry and dead animals.
- Keep dogs and children from playing in sand and soil.
- Kennel dogs on cement or gravel; avoid dirt runs.
- Administer heartworm preventives regularly.
- Have your vet examine your dog's stools at your annual visits.
- Select a boarding kennel carefully so as to avoid contamination from other dogs or an unsanitary environment.
- Prevent dogs from roaming. Obey local leash laws.

months as well. Unfortunately, since dogs don't develop resistance to whipworms, it is difficult to prevent them from getting reinfected if they visit soil contaminated with whipworm eggs.

TAPEWORMS

There are many different species of tapeworm that affect dogs, but *Dipylidium caninum* is probably the most common and is spread by fleas. Flea larvae feed on organic debris and tapeworm eggs in the environment and, when a dog chews at himself and manages to ingest fleas, he might get a dose of tapeworm at the same time. The tapeworm then develops further in the intestine of the dog.

The tapeworm itself, which is a parasitic flatworm that latches onto the intestinal wall, is composed of numerous segments. When the segments break off into the intestine (as proglottids), they may accumulate around the rectum, like grains of rice. While this tapeworm is disgusting in its behavior, it is not directly communicable to humans (although humans can also get infected by swallowing fleas).

A much more dangerous flatworm is *Echinococcus multilocularis*, which is typically found in foxes, coyotes and wolves. The eggs are passed in the feces and infect rodents, and, when dogs eat the rodents, the dogs can be infected by thousands of adult tapeworms. While the parasites don't cause many problems in dogs, this is considered the most lethal worm infection that people can get. Take appropriate precautions if you live in an area in which these tapeworms are found. Do not use mulch that may contain feces of dogs, cats or wildlife, and discourage your pets from hunting

wildlife. Treat these tapeworm infections aggressively in pets, because if humans get infected, approximately half die.

HEARTWORMS

Heartworm disease is caused by the parasite *Dirofilaria immitis* and is seen in dogs around the world. A member of the roundworm group, it is spread between dogs by the bite of an infected mosquito. The mosquito injects infective larvae into the dog's skin with its bite, and these larvae develop under the skin for a period of time before making their way to the heart. There they develop into adults, which grow and create blockages of the heart, lungs and major blood vessels there. They also start producing offspring (microfilariae)

A dog tapeworm proglottid (body segment).

The dog tapeworm *Taenia pisiformis.*

S. E. M. BY DR. DENNIS KUNKEL, UNIVERSITY OF HAWAII.

A Look at Internal Parasites

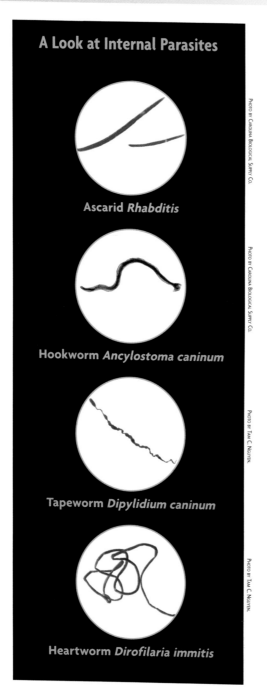

PHOTO BY CAROLINA BIOLOGICAL SUPPLY CO.

Ascarid *Rhabditis*

PHOTO BY CAROLINA BIOLOGICAL SUPPLY CO.

Hookworm *Ancylostoma caninum*

PHOTO BY TAM C. NGUYEN.

Tapeworm *Dipylidium caninum*

PHOTO BY TAM C. NGUYEN.

Heartworm *Dirofilaria immitis*

and these microfilariae circulate in the bloodstream, waiting to hitch a ride when the next mosquito bites. Once in the mosquito, the microfilariae develop into infective larvae and the entire process is repeated.

When dogs get infected with heartworm, over time they tend to develop symptoms associated with heart disease, such as coughing, exercise intolerance and potentially many other manifestations. Diagnosis is confirmed by either seeing the microfilariae themselves in blood samples or using immunologic tests (antigen testing) to identify the presence of adult heartworms. Since antigen tests measure the presence of adult heartworms and microfilarial tests measure offspring produced by adults, neither are positive until six to seven months after the initial infection. However, the beginning of damage can occur by fifth-stage larvae as early as three months after infection. Thus it is possible for dogs to be harboring problem-causing larvae for up to three months before either type of test would identify an infection.

The good news is that there are great protocols available for preventing heartworm in dogs. Testing is critical in the process, and it is important to understand the benefits as well as the limitations of such testing. All dogs six months of age or older that have not been on continuous heartworm-preventive medication should be

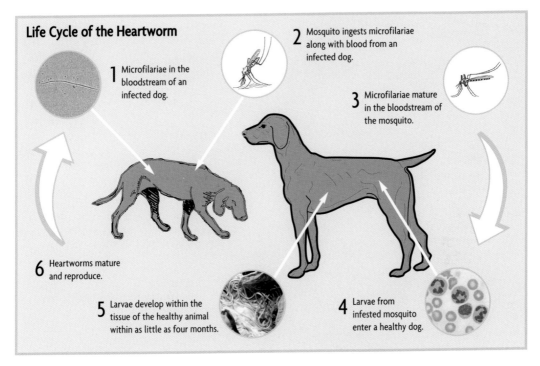

Life Cycle of the Heartworm

1 Microfilariae in the bloodstream of an infected dog.

2 Mosquito ingests microfilariae along with blood from an infected dog.

3 Microfilariae mature in the bloodstream of the mosquito.

6 Heartworms mature and reproduce.

5 Larvae develop within the tissue of the healthy animal within as little as four months.

4 Larvae from infested mosquito enter a healthy dog.

screened with microfilarial or anti-gen tests. For dogs receiving preventive medication, periodic antigen testing helps assess the effectiveness of the preventives. The American Heartworm Society guidelines suggest that annual retesting may not be necessary when owners have absolutely provided continuous heartworm prevention. Retesting on a two- to three-year interval may be sufficient in these cases. However, your veterinarian will likely have specific guidelines under which heartworm preventives will be prescribed, and many prefer to err on the side of safety and retest annually.

It is indeed fortunate that heartworm is relatively easy to prevent, because treatments can be as life-threatening as the disease itself. Treatment requires a two-step process that kills the adult heartworms first and then the microfilariae. Prevention is obviously preferable; this involves a once-monthly oral or topical treatment. The most common oral preventives include ivermectin (not suitable for some breeds), moxidectin and milbe-mycin oxime; the once-a-month topical drug selamectin provides heartworm protection in addition to flea, tick and other parasite controls.

THE ABCs OF Emergency Care

Abrasions

Clean wound with running water or 3% hydrogen peroxide. Pat dry with gauze and spray with antibiotic. Do not cover.

Animal Bites

Clean area with soap and saline solution or water. Apply pressure to any bleeding area. Apply antibiotic ointment. Identify biting animal and contact vet.

Antifreeze Poisoning

Induce vomiting and take dog to the vet.

Bee Sting

Remove stinger and apply soothing lotion or cold compress; give antihistamine in proper dosage.

Bleeding

Apply pressure directly to wound with gauze or towel for five to ten minutes. If wound does not stop bleeding, wrap wound with gauze and adhesive tape.

Bloat/Gastric Torsion

Immediately take the dog to the vet or emergency clinic; phone from car. No time to waste.

Burns

Chemical: Bathe dog with water and pet shampoo. Rinse in saline solution. Apply antibiotic ointment.

Acid: Rinse with water. Apply one part baking soda, two parts water to affected area.

Alkali: Rinse with water. Apply one part vinegar, four parts water to affected area.

Electrical: Apply antibiotic ointment. Seek veterinary assistance immediately.

Choking

If the dog is on the verge of collapsing, wedge a solid object, such as the handle of a screwdriver, between molars on one side of mouth to keep mouth open. Pull tongue out. Use long-nosed pliers or fingers to remove foreign object. Do not push the object down the dog's throat. For small or medium dogs, hold dog upside down by hind legs and shake firmly to dislodge foreign object.

Chlorine Ingestion

With clean water, rinse the mouth and eyes. Give dog water to drink; contact the vet.

Constipation

Feed dog 2 tablespoons bran flakes with each meal. Encourage drinking water. Mix 1/4-teaspoon mineral oil in dog's food.

Diarrhea

Withhold food for 12 to 24 hours. Feed dog anti-diarrheal with eyedropper. When feeding resumes, feed one part boiled hamburger, one part plain cooked rice, 1/4 to 3/4 cup four times daily.

Dog Bite

Snip away hair around puncture wound; clean with 3% hydrogen peroxide; apply tincture of iodine. Identify biting dog and call the vet. If wound appears deep, take the dog to the vet.

Frostbite

Wrap the dog in a heavy blanket. Warm affected area with a warm bath for ten minutes. Red color to skin will return with circulation; if tissues are pale after 20 minutes, contact the vet.

Use a portable, durable container large enough to contain all items.

Heat Stroke
Submerge the dog (up to his muzzle) in cold water; if no response within ten minutes, contact the vet.

Hot Spots
Mix 2 packets Domeboro® with 2 cups water. Saturate cloth with mixture and apply to hot spots for 15–30 minutes. Apply antibiotic ointment. Repeat every six to eight hours.

Poisonous Plants
Wash affected area with soap and water. Cleanse with alcohol. For foxtail/grass, apply antibiotic ointment. Contact vet if plant is ingested.

Rat Poison Ingestion
Induce vomiting. Keep dog calm, maintain dog's normal body temperature (use blanket or heating pad). Get to the vet for antidote.

Shock
Keep the dog calm and warm; call for veterinary assistance.

Snake Bite
If possible, bandage the area and apply pressure. If the area is not conducive to bandaging, use ice to control bleeding. Get immediate help from the vet.

Tick Removal
Apply flea and tick spray directly on tick. Wait one minute. Using tweezers or wearing plastic gloves, grasp the tick's body firmly. Apply antibiotic ointment.

Vomiting
Restrict water intake; offer a few ice cubes. Withhold food for next meal. Contact vet if vomiting (or diarrhea/constipation) persists longer than 24 hours.

DOG OWNER'S FIRST-AID KIT
- ❏ **Gauze bandages/swabs**
- ❏ **Adhesive and non-adhesive bandages**
- ❏ **Antibiotic powder**
- ❏ **Antiseptic wash**
- ❏ **Hydrogen peroxide 3%**
- ❏ **Antibiotic ointment**
- ❏ **Lubricating jelly**
- ❏ **Rectal thermometer**
- ❏ **Nylon muzzle**
- ❏ **Scissors and forceps**
- ❏ **Eyedropper**
- ❏ **Syringe**
- ❏ **Anti-bacterial/fungal solution**
- ❏ **Saline solution**
- ❏ **Antihistamine**
- ❏ **Cotton balls**
- ❏ **Nail clippers**
- ❏ **Screwdriver/pen knife**
- ❏ **Flashlight**
- ❏ **Emergency phone numbers**

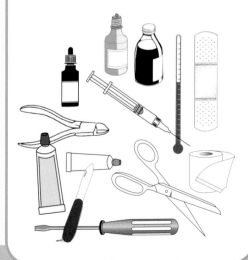

Number-One Killer Disease in Dogs: CANCER

In every age, there is a word associated with a disease or plague that causes humans to shudder. In the 21st century, that word is "cancer." Just as cancer is the leading cause of death in humans, it claims nearly half the lives of dogs that die from a natural disease as well as half the dogs that die over the age of ten years.

Described as a genetic disease, cancer becomes a greater risk as the dog ages. Vets and dog owners have become increasingly aware of the threat of cancer to dogs. Statistics reveal that one dog in every five will develop cancer, the most common of which is skin cancer. Many cancers, including prostate, ovarian and breast cancer, can be avoided by spaying and neutering our dogs by the age of six months.

Early detection of cancer can save or extend a dog's life, so it is absolutely vital for owners to have their dogs examined by a qualified vet or oncologist immediately upon detection of any abnormality. Certain dietary guidelines have also proven to reduce the onset and spread of cancer. Foods based on fish rather than beef, due to the presence of Omega-3 fatty acids, are recommended. Other amino acids such as glutamine have significant benefits for canines, particularly those breeds that show a greater susceptibility to cancer.

Cancer management and treatments promise hope for future generations of canines. Since the disease is genetic, breeders should never breed a dog whose parents, grandparents and any related siblings have developed cancer. It is difficult to know whether to exclude an otherwise healthy dog from a breeding program, as the disease does not manifest itself until the dog's senior years.

RECOGNIZE CANCER WARNING SIGNS

Since early detection can possibly rescue your dog from becoming a cancer statistic, it is essential for owners to recognize the possible signs and seek the assistance of a qualified professional.

- Abnormal bumps or lumps that continue to grow
- Bleeding or discharge from any body cavity
- Persistent stiffness or lameness
- Recurrent sores or sores that do not heal
- Inappetence
- Breathing difficulties
- Weight loss
- Bad breath or odors
- General malaise and fatigue
- Eating and swallowing problems
- Difficulty urinating and defecating

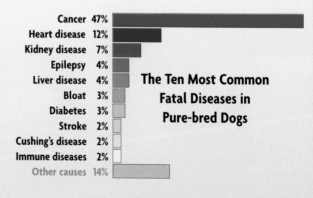

Cancer	47%
Heart disease	12%
Kidney disease	7%
Epilepsy	4%
Liver disease	4%
Bloat	3%
Diabetes	3%
Stroke	2%
Cushing's disease	2%
Immune diseases	2%
Other causes	14%

The Ten Most Common Fatal Diseases in Pure-bred Dogs

CDS: Cognitive Dysfunction Syndrome

"Old-Dog Syndrome"

There are many ways for you to evaluate old-dog syndrome. Veterinarians have defined CDS (cognitive dysfunction syndrome) as the gradual deterioration of cognitive abilities, indicated by changes in the dog's behavior. When a dog changes his routine response, and maladies have been eliminated as the cause of these behavioral changes, then CDS is the usual diagnosis.

More than half the dogs over eight years old suffer from some form of CDS. The older the dog, the more chance he has of suffering from CDS. In humans, doctors often dismiss the CDS behavioral changes as part of "winding down."

There are four major signs of CDS: frequent potty accidents inside the home, sleeping much more or much less than normal, acting confused and failing to respond to social stimuli.

Symptoms of CDS

FREQUENT POTTY ACCIDENTS

- Urinates in the house.
- Defecates in the house.
- Doesn't signal that he wants to go out.

FAILURE TO RESPOND TO SOCIAL STIMULI

- Comes to people less frequently, whether called or not.
- Doesn't tolerate petting for more than a short time.
- Doesn't come to the door when you return home.

CONFUSION

- Goes outside and just stands there.
- Appears confused with a faraway look in his eyes.
- Hides more often.
- Doesn't recognize friends.
- Doesn't come when called.
- Walks around listlessly and without a destination.

SLEEP PATTERNS

- Awakens more slowly.
- Sleeps more than normal during the day.
- Sleeps less during the night.

Is dog showing in your blood? Are you excited by the idea of gaiting your handsome Irish Wolfhound around the ring to the thunderous applause of an enthusiastic audience? Are you certain that your beloved Irish Wolfhound is flawless? You are not alone! Every loving owner thinks that his dog has no faults, or too few to mention. No matter how many times an owner reads the breed standard, he cannot find any faults in his aristocratic companion dog. If this sounds like you, and if you are considering entering your Irish Wolfhound in a dog show, here are some basic questions to ask yourself:

• Did you purchase a "show-quality" puppy from the breeder?
• Is your puppy at least six months of age?
• Does the puppy exhibit correct show type for his breed?
• Does your puppy have any disqualifying faults?
• Is your Irish Wolfhound registered with the American Kennel Club?
• How much time do you have to devote to training, grooming, conditioning and exhibiting your dog?
• Do you understand the rules and regulations of a dog show?
• Do you have time to learn how to show your dog properly?
• Do you have the financial resources to invest in showing your dog?
• Will you show the dog yourself or hire a professional handler?
• Do you have a vehicle that can accommodate your weekend trips to the dog shows?

Success in the show ring requires more than a pretty face, a waggy tail and a pocketful of liver. Even though dog shows can be exciting and enjoyable, the sport of conformation makes great demands on the exhibitors and the dogs. Winning exhibitors live for their dogs, devoting time and

AKC GROUPS
For showing purposes, the American Kennel Club divides its recognized breeds into seven groups: Hounds, Sporting Dogs, Working Dogs, Terriers, Toys, Non-Sporting Dogs and Herding Dogs.

money to their dogs' presentation, conditioning and training. Very few novices, even those with good dogs, will find themselves in the winners' circle, though it does happen. Don't be disheartened, though. Every exhibitor began as a novice and worked his way up to the Group ring. It's the "working your way up" part that you must keep in mind.

Assuming that you have purchased a puppy of the correct type and quality for showing, let's begin to examine the world of showing and what's required to get started. Although the entry fee into a dog show is nominal, there are lots of other hidden costs involved with "finishing" your Irish Wolfhound, that is, making him a champion. Things like equipment, travel, training and conditioning all cost money. A more serious campaign will include fees for a professional handler, boarding, cross-country travel and advertising. Top-winning show dogs can represent a very considerable investment— over $100,000 has been spent in campaigning some dogs. (The investment can be less, of course, for owners who don't use professional handlers.)

Many owners, on the other hand, enter their "average" Irish Wolfhounds in dog shows for the fun and enjoyment of it. Dog showing makes an absorbing hobby, with many rewards for

dogs and owners alike. If you're having fun, meeting other people who share your interests and enjoying the overall experience, you likely will catch the "bug." Once the dog-show bug bites, its effects can last a lifetime; it's certainly much better than a deer tick! Soon you will be envisioning yourself in the center ring at the Westminster Kennel Club Dog Show in New York City, competing for the prestigious Best in Show cup. This magical dog show is televised annually from Madison Square Garden, and the victorious dog becomes a celebrity overnight.

Each dog's gait is evaluated in the show ring so that the judge can assess structure and movement as typical of the breed.

AKC CONFORMATION BASICS

Visiting a dog show as a spectator is a great place to start. Pick up the show catalog to find out what time your breed is being shown, who is judging the breed and in

should decide how each dog stacks up (conforms) to the breed standard for his given breed: how well does this Irish Wolfhound conform to the ideal representative detailed in the standard? Ideally, this is what happens. In reality, however, this ideal often gets slighted as the judge compares Irish Wolfhound #1 to Irish Wolfhound #2. Again, the ideal is that each dog is judged based on his merits in comparison to his breed standard, not in comparison to the other dogs in the ring. It is easier for judges to

A true celebration of the occasion—showing Irish Wolfhounds in Ireland on the feast of the great St. Patrick. This winner of the St. Patrick's Day Show sponsored by the Irish Kennel Club is a marvelously proportioned dog.

which ring the classes will be held. To start, Irish Wolfhounds compete against other Irish Wolfhounds, and the winner is selected as Best of Breed by the judge. This is the procedure for each breed. At a group show, all of the Best of Breed winners go on to compete for Group One in their respective groups. For example, all Best of Breed winners in a given group compete against each other; this is done for all seven groups. Finally, all seven group winners go head to head in the ring for the Best in Show award.

What most spectators don't understand is the basic idea of conformation. A dog show is often referred as a "conformation" show. This means that the judge

MEET THE AKC

The American Kennel Club is the main governing body of the dog sport in the United States. Founded in 1884, the AKC consists of 500 or more independent dog clubs plus 4,500 affiliated clubs, all of which follow the AKC rules and regulations. Additionally, the AKC maintains a registry for pure-bred dogs in the US and works to preserve the integrity of the sport and its continuation in the country. Over 1,000,000 dogs are registered each year, representing about 150 recognized breeds. There are over 15,000 competitive events held annually for which over 2,000,000 dogs enter to participate. Dogs compete to earn over 40 different titles, from champion to Companion Dog to Master Agility Champion.

compare dogs of the same breed to decide which they think is the better specimen; in the Group and Best in Show ring, however, it is very difficult to compare one breed to another, like apples to oranges. Thus the dog's conformation to the breed standard—not to mention advertising dollars and good handling—is essential to success in conformation shows. The dog described in the standard (the standard for each AKC breed is written and approved by the breed's national parent club and then submitted to the AKC for approval) is the perfect dog of that breed, and breeders keep their eye on the standard when they choose which dogs to breed, hoping to get closer and closer to the ideal with each litter.

Another good first step for the novice is to join a dog club. You will be astonished by the many and different kinds of dog clubs in the country, with about 5,000 clubs holding events every year. Most clubs require that prospective new members present two letters of recommendation from existing members. Perhaps you've made some friends visiting a show held by a particular club and you would like to join that club. Dog clubs may specialize in a single breed, like a local or regional Irish Wolfhound club, or in a specific pursuit, such as obedience, tracking or lure-coursing events. There are all-breed

clubs for all dog enthusiasts; they sponsor special training days, seminars on topics like grooming or handling or lectures on breeding or canine genetics. There are also clubs that specialize in certain types of dogs, like sighthounds, hunting dogs, companion dogs, etc.

A parent club is the national organization, sanctioned by the AKC, which promotes and safeguards its breed in the country. The Irish Wolfhound Club of America was formed in 1926 and can be contacted on the Internet at

With his impressive stature and dignified bearing, along with his distinguished good looks, the Irish Wolfhound is quite a sight in the show ring.

FIVE CLASSES AT SHOWS

At most AKC all-breed shows, there are five regular classes offered: Puppy, Novice, Bred-by-Exhibitor, American-bred and Open. The Puppy Class is usually divided as 6 to 9 months of age and 9 to 12 months of age. When deciding in which class to enter your dog, whether male or female, you must carefully check the show schedule to make sure that you have selected the right class. Depending on the age of the dog, previous first-place wins and the sex of the dog, you must make the best choice. It is possible to enter a one-year-old dog who has not won sufficient first places in any of the non-Puppy Classes, though the competition is more intense the further you progress from the Puppy Class.

www.iwclubofamerica.org. The parent club holds an annual national specialty show, usually in a different city each year, in which many of the country's top dogs, handlers and breeders gather to compete. At a specialty show, only members of a single breed are invited to participate. There are also group specialties, in which all members of a group are invited. For more information about dog clubs in your area, contact the AKC at www.akc.org on the Internet or write them at 5580 Centerview Drive, Raleigh, NC 27606-3390.

OTHER TYPES OF COMPETITION

In addition to conformation shows, the AKC holds a variety of other competitive events. Obedience trials, agility trials and tracking trials are open to all breeds, while hunting tests, field trials, lure coursing, herding tests and trials, earthdog tests and coonhound events are limited to specific breeds or groups of breeds. The Junior Showmanship program is offered to aspiring young handlers and their dogs, and the Canine Good Citizen® Program is an all-around good-behavior test open to all dogs, pure-bred and mixed.

OBEDIENCE TRIALS

Mrs. Helen Whitehouse Walker, a Standard Poodle fancier, can be credited with introducing obedience trials to the United States. In the 1930s she designed a series of exercises based on those of the Associated Sheep, Police, Army Dog Society of Great Britain. These exercises were intended to evaluate the working relationship between dog and owner. Since those early days of the sport in the US, obedience trials have grown more and more popular, and now more than 2,000 trials each year attract over 100,000 dogs and their owners. Any dog registered with the AKC, regardless of neutering or other disqualifications that would preclude entry in conformation competition, can participate in obedience trials.

There are three levels of difficulty in obedience competition. The first (and easiest) level is the Novice, in which dogs can earn the Companion Dog (CD) title. The intermediate level is the Open level, in which the Companion Dog Excellent (CDX) title is awarded. The advanced level is the Utility level, in which dogs compete for the Utility Dog (UD) title. Classes at each level are further divided into "A" and "B," with "A" for beginners and "B" for those with more experience. In order to win a title at a given level, a dog must earn three "legs." A "leg" is accomplished when a dog scores 170 or higher (200 is a perfect score). The scoring system gets a little trickier when you understand that a dog must score more than 50% of the points available for each exercise in order to actually earn the points. Available points for each exercise range between 20 and 40.

Once he's earned the UD title, a dog can go on to win the prestigious title of Utility Dog Excellent (UDX) by winning "legs" in ten shows. Additionally, Utility Dogs who win "legs" in Open B and Utility B earn points toward the lofty title of Obedience Trial Champion (OTCh.). Established in 1977 by the AKC, this title requires a dog to earn 100 points as well as three first places in a combination of Open B and Utility B classes under three different judges. The "brass ring" of obedience competition is the AKC's National Obedience Invitational. This is an exclusive competition for only the cream of the obedience crop. In order to qualify for the invitational, a dog must be ranked in either the top 25 all-breeds in obedience or in the top three for his breed in obedience. The title at stake here is that of National Obedience Champion (NOC).

AGILITY TRIALS

Agility trials became sanctioned by the AKC in August 1994, when the first licensed agility trials were held. Since that time, agility certainly has grown in popularity by leaps and bounds, literally! The AKC allows all registered breeds (including Miscellaneous Class breeds) to participate, providing the dog is 12 months of age or older. Agility is designed so that the handler demonstrates how well the dog can work at his side. The handler directs his dog through, over, under and around an obstacle course that includes jumps, tires, the dog walk, weave poles, pipe tunnels, collapsed tunnels and more. While working his way through the course, the dog must keep one eye and ear on the handler and the rest of his body on the course. The handler runs along with the dog, giving verbal and hand signals to guide the dog through the course.

The first organization to promote agility trials in the US was the United States Dog Agility Association, Inc. (USDAA). Established in 1986, the USDAA sparked the formation of many member clubs around the country. To participate in USDAA trials, dogs must be at least 18 months of age.

The USDAA and AKC both offer titles to winning dogs, although the exercises and requirements of the two organizations differ. Agility trials are a great way to keep your dog active, and they will keep you running, too! You should join a local agility club to learn more about the sport. These clubs offer sessions in which you can introduce your dog to the various obstacles as well as training classes to prepare him for competition. In no time, your dog will be climbing A-frames, crossing the dog walk and flying over hurdles, all with you right beside him. Your heart will leap every time your dog jumps through the hoop—and you'll be having just as much (if not more) fun!

LURE COURSING

Owners of sighthound breeds have the opportunity to participate in lure coursing. Lure-coursing events are exciting and fast-paced, requiring dogs to follow an artificial lure around a course on an open field. Scores are based on the dog's speed, enthusiasm, agility, endurance and ability to follow the lure. At

CANINE GOOD CITIZEN® PROGRAM

Have you ever considered getting your dog "certified"? The AKC's Canine Good Citizen® Program affords your dog just that opportunity. Your dog shows that he is a well-behaved canine citizen, using the basic training and good manners you have taught him, by taking a series of ten tests that illustrate that he can behave properly at home, in a public place and around other dogs. The tests are administered by participating dog clubs, colleges, 4-H clubs, Scouts and other community groups and are open to all pure-bred and mixed-breed dogs. Upon passing the ten tests, the suffix CGC is then applied to your dog's name.

The ten tests are: 1. Accepting a friendly stranger; 2. Sitting politely for petting; 3. Appearance and grooming; 4. Walking on a lead; 5. Walking through a group of people; 6. Sit, down and stay on command; 7. Coming when called; 8. Meeting another dog; 9. Calm reaction to distractions; 10. Separation from owner.

the non-competitive level, lure coursing is designed to gauge a sighthound's instinctive coursing ability. Competitive lure coursing is more demanding, requiring training and conditioning for a dog to develop his coursing instincts and skills to the fullest, thus preserving the intended function of all sighthound breeds. Breeds eligible for AKC lure coursing are the Irish Wolfhound, Whippet, Basenji, Greyhound, Italian Greyhound, Afghan Hound, Borzoi, Ibizan Hound, Pharaoh Hound, Scottish Deerhound, Saluki and Rhodesian Ridgeback.

Lure coursing on a competitive level is certainly wonderful physical and mental exercise for a dog. A dog must be at least one year of age to enter an AKC coursing event, and he must not have any disqualifications according to his breed standard. Check the AKC's rules and regulations for details. To get started, you can consult the AKC's website to help you find a coursing club in your area. A club can introduce you to the sport and help you learn how to train your dog correctly.

Titles awarded in lure coursing are Junior Courser (JC), Senior Courser (SC) and Master Courser (MC); these are suffix titles, affixed to the end of the dog's name. The Field Champion (FC) title is a prefix title, affixed

> **TRACKING**
> Tracking tests are exciting ways to test your Irish Wolfhound's instinctive scenting ability on a competitive level. All dogs have a nose, and all breeds are welcome in tracking tests. The first AKC-licensed tracking test took place in 1937 as part of the Utility level at an obedience trial, and thus competitive tracking was officially begun. The first title, Tracking Dog (TD), was offered in 1947, ten years after the first official tracking test. It was not until 1980 that the AKC added the title Tracking Dog Excellent (TDX), which was followed by the title Versatile Surface Tracking (VST) in 1995. Champion Tracker (CT) is awarded to a dog who has earned all three of those titles.

to the beginning of the dog's name. A Dual Champion is a hound that has earned both a Field Champion title as well as a show championship. A Triple Champion (TC) title is awarded to a dog that is a Champion, Field Champion and Obedience Trial Champion. The suffix Lure Courser Excellent (LCX) is given to a dog who has earned the FC title plus 45 additional championship points, and number designations are added to the title upon each additional 45 championship points earned (LCX II, III, IV and so on).

The appeal of lure-coursing is seeing these beautiful hounds, with their remarkable speed and graceful movement, performing at what they instinctively do best.

Sighthounds also can participate in events sponsored by the American Sighthound Field Association (ASFA), an organization devoted to the pursuit of lure coursing. The ASFA was founded in 1972 as a means of keeping open field coursing dogs fit in the off-season. It has grown into the largest lure-coursing association in the world. Dogs must be of an accepted sighthound breed in order to be eligible for participation. Each dog must pass a certification run in which he shows that he can run with another dog without interfering. The course is laid out using pulleys and a motor to drive the string around the pulleys. Normally white plastic bags are used as lures, although real fur strips may also be attached. Dogs run in trios, each handled by their own slipper. The dogs are scored on their endurance, follow, speed, agility and enthusiasm. Dogs earn their Field Champion titles by earning two first places, or one first- and two second-place finishes, as well as accumulating 100 points. They can then go on to earn the LCM title, Lure Courser of Merit, by winning four first places and accumulating 300 additional points.

Coursing is an all-day event, held in all weather conditions. It is great fun for the whole family, but on a rainy, cold day, it's best to leave the kids at home!

RACING

The Large Gazehound Racing Association (LGRA) and the National Oval Track Racing Association (NOTRA) are organizations that sponsor and regulate dog races. Races are usually either 200-yard sprints (LGRA) or semi- or complete ovals (NOTRA). Both of these organizations allow most sighthound breeds except Whippets to participate. (Whippets have their own racing organizations exclusively for the breed.) In both LGRA and NOTRA races, the dogs generally run out of starting boxes, meaning that racing dogs must be trained to the box. Local racing clubs offer training programs that can assist novice owners and dogs.

Dogs compete in a draw of four each and are ranked according to their previous racing record. The lure in LGRA events consists of both real fur and a predator call. In NOTRA events, the lure is white plastic and often a fur strip. There are three programs and the dogs are rotated through the draw according to their finish in each preceding program. Dogs earn the Gazehound Racing Champion (GRC) or the Oval Racing Champion (ORC) title when they accumulate 15 race points. Dogs can go on to earn the Superior titles by accumulating 30 additional points.

Both LGRA and NOTRA races are owner-participation sports in which each owner plays some

role: catcher, walker, line judge or foul judge. If you plan to race your dog, plan to work all day during a race day! There is little time for anything else, but the reward of seeing four dogs pour over the finish line shoulder to shoulder is more than enough.

The stake begins as the dogs are "slipped" by their handlers.

Lure-coursing stakes are typically run in trios, with dogs designated by different colors, usually blue, pink and yellow.

INDEX

*Page numbers in **boldface** indicate illustrations.*

My Irish Wolfhound

PUT YOUR PUPPY'S FIRST PICTURE HERE

Dog's Name _____

Date _____ Photographer _____